**COUNCIL** *on*
**FOREIGN**
**RELATIONS**

*Council Special Report No. 84*
*April 2019*

# Trump's Foreign Policies Are Better Than They Seem

Robert D. Blackwill

The Council on Foreign Relations (CFR) is an independent, nonpartisan membership organization, think tank, and publisher dedicated to being a resource for its members, government officials, business executives, journalists, educators and students, civic and religious leaders, and other interested citizens in order to help them better understand the world and the foreign policy choices facing the United States and other countries. Founded in 1921, CFR carries out its mission by maintaining a diverse membership, with special programs to promote interest and develop expertise in the next generation of foreign policy leaders; convening meetings at its headquarters in New York and in Washington, DC, and other cities where senior government officials, members of Congress, global leaders, and prominent thinkers come together with Council members to discuss and debate major international issues; supporting a Studies Program that fosters independent research, enabling CFR scholars to produce articles, reports, and books and hold roundtables that analyze foreign policy issues and make concrete policy recommendations; publishing *Foreign Affairs*, the preeminent journal on international affairs and U.S. foreign policy; sponsoring Independent Task Forces that produce reports with both findings and policy prescriptions on the most important foreign policy topics; and providing up-to-date information and analysis about world events and American foreign policy on its website, CFR.org.

**The Council on Foreign Relations takes no institutional positions on policy issues and has no affiliation with the U.S. government. All views expressed in its publications and on its website are the sole responsibility of the author or authors.**

Council Special Reports (CSRs) are concise policy briefs, produced to provide a rapid response to a developing crisis or contribute to the public's understanding of current policy dilemmas. CSRs are written by individual authors—who may be CFR fellows or acknowledged experts from outside the institution—in consultation with an advisory committee, and are intended to take sixty days from inception to publication. The committee serves as a sounding board and provides feedback on a draft report. It usually meets twice—once before a draft is written and once again when there is a draft for review; however, advisory committee members, unlike Task Force members, are not asked to sign off on the report or to otherwise endorse it. Once published, CSRs are posted on CFR.org.

For further information about CFR or this Special Report, please write to the Council on Foreign Relations, 58 East 68th Street, New York, NY 10065, or call the Communications office at 212.434.9888. Visit our website, CFR.org.

To submit a letter in response to a Council Special Report for publication on our website, CFR.org, you may send an email to publications@cfr.org. Alternatively, letters may be mailed to us at: Publications Department, Council on Foreign Relations, 58 East 68th Street, New York, NY 10065. Letters should include the writer's name, postal address, and daytime phone number. Letters may be edited for length and clarity, and may be published online. Please do not send attachments. All letters become the property of the Council on Foreign Relations and will not be returned. We regret that, owing to the volume of correspondence, we cannot respond to every letter.

This report is printed on paper that is FSC ® Chain-of-Custody Certified by a printer who is certified by BM TRADA North America Inc.

MIX
Paper from
responsible sources
FSC
www.fsc.org
FSC® C101537

# CONTENTS

iv    *Foreword*
vi    *Acknowledgments*

2    Introduction
8    China
18    Climate Change
21    North Korea
27    NATO and European Security
32    Russia
39    Iran
42    Syria
44    Saudi Arabia
47    Israel
49    Afghanistan
54    India
57    Venezuela
59    Trade
65    Conclusion: Grade for Trump's Overall Foreign Policy

69    *Endnotes*
104    *About the Author*

# FOREWORD

It is not easy to attempt a fair assessment of President Donald J. Trump's foreign policy. In part this is because of circumstances, namely that we are just past the halfway mark of his term, which began in January 2017. "Incomplete" is on one level the only appropriate mark.

But the difficulty in assessing this president also reflects the style of his foreign policy, including the frequent recourse to social media, the secrecy that has surrounded critical summits, the high turnover of senior-level officials, and the gaps that often appear between the positions of these aides and the president. It can be difficult to keep up and to be confident as to just what foreign policy is being implemented.

In this new Council Special Report, however, Henry A. Kissinger Senior Fellow for U.S. Foreign Policy Robert D. Blackwill attempts just such an assessment. He goes about it the right way, evaluating President Trump's foreign policy not against his and his administration's rhetoric but against its impact on the U.S. national interest.

Blackwill examines President Trump's actions in important policy areas, including ties with allies, relations with China and Russia, and policies toward the Middle East, North Korea, Venezuela, trade, and climate change. He then grades each of the president's major foreign policies and offers an overall assessment of the quality of the Trump administration's foreign policy halfway through its first term.

Blackwill argues that even though many of President Trump's actions have been impetuous and the president oversees a chaotic and often dysfunctional policymaking process, some of his individual foreign policies are better than his critics give him credit for. Blackwill points to what he sees as a much-needed toughening of U.S. policy toward China, a justified U.S. withdrawal from Syria and disengagement from Afghanistan, and closer relations with India, Israel, and

Saudi Arabia. History teaches us, according to Blackwill, that "flawed individuals and policy processes sometimes produce successful results." Like Wagner's music, he argues, Trump's foreign policy is better than it sounds.

For some readers, I expect Blackwill's grades will be too low, while for others, his grades will not be low enough. I agree with Blackwill that the president has been right to challenge China on its actions in the trade realm, in what he has done to rally regional and international support against the Nicolas Maduro regime in Venezuela, and in cultivating closer ties with India. But I would give President Trump a lower grade on how he has handled Iran, North Korea, and Syria. In addition, it is hard to see what the Trump administration has received in exchange for its uncritical embrace of Saudi Arabia and Crown Prince Mohammed bin Salman or for moving the U.S. embassy in Israel to Jerusalem.

But these and other differences I have or others will have with Ambassador Blackwill's assessments overlook the fundamental value of this rigorous study undertaken by an experienced scholar-practitioner. It is the sort of work that is all too rare in this politicized environment we live in and where 280 characters often substitute for in-depth analysis. There is much of value to learn in the pages to follow, and I urge readers to make their way through this paper and come to their own conclusions as to what grade the forty-fifth president deserves so far for his foreign policy.

**Richard N. Haass**
*President*
Council on Foreign Relations
April 2019

# ACKNOWLEDGMENTS

This Council Special Report greatly benefited from the dozens of specific suggestions and valuable improvements by Henry Kissinger, Graham Allison, Hal Brands, Frank Gavin, Philip Zelikow, and Robert Zoellick. I took most of their suggested fixes but, as they will see, not all. I am especially grateful to Dr. Kissinger for his friendship, inspiration, and guidance throughout virtually my entire adult life. I also thank Council on Foreign Relations (CFR) President Richard N. Haass and Senior Vice President and Director of Studies James M. Lindsay for their review and comments. I appreciate the work of the CFR Publications team, Patricia Lee Dorff, Julie Hersh, Chloe Moffett, and Sumit Poudyal, for editorial contributions. My special thanks go to Theodore Rappleye, my brilliant and inexhaustible research associate, and to his successor, Daniel Clay. Without Ted's voluminous research, this report would still be an incomplete draft searching for citations.

The analysis and conclusions of the report are my responsibility alone.

**Robert D. Blackwill**

What is new about the emerging world order is that, for the first time, the United States can neither withdraw from the world nor dominate it.

—Henry Kissinger, *Diplomacy*, 1994

# INTRODUCTION

President Donald J. Trump's actions have often been rash, ignorant, and chaotic. He seems sometimes to imagine that he can withdraw from the world and sometimes to think he can dominate it. Yet some of his individual foreign policies are substantially better than his opponents assert.[1]

It is no wonder that Trump is not given sufficient credit for his foreign policies. After more than two tumultuous years in office, the president has disrupted a whole series of conventions in the international system, some of them undoubtedly needed, but adopted few follow-on strategies and little or no implementation. If Trump believes that he was elected to "bust things up," as former State Department Counselor and National Security Council official Philip Zelikow has put it, he is succeeding.[2] According to the *Washington Post*, Trump has spoken or written more than nine thousand untruths and misrepresentations.[3] He conveys foreign policy failures as successes and minor accomplishments as cosmic victories. He makes important decisions against the advice of his cabinet advisors—if he consults them at all. He has had unprecedented turnover in senior foreign and defense policy positions and, at this writing, has had three national security advisors. In sum, there is no steady interagency decision-making process within the administration because the president apparently does not believe that he needs one.[4] He treats international negotiation as a form of demolition derby.

Trump has insulted many of the leaders of America's closest friends, including Emmanuel Macron of France, Angela Merkel of Germany, and Theresa May of the United Kingdom. At the same time, he has regularly praised autocrats—Jair Bolsonaro of Brazil, Xi Jinping of China, Viktor Orban of Hungary, Kim Jong-un of North Korea, Vladimir Putin of Russia, Recep Tayyip Erdogan of Turkey, and more.[5] He has disrupted relations with Canada and Mexico, treating them as adversaries rather than friendly neighbors. The president has threatened to pull out of the North Atlantic Treaty Organization (NATO) and has called into question whether the United States would fulfill its treaty obligations and come to the aid of its European allies if they were attacked. He has doubted the value of U.S. alliances in ways not shared by any of his predecessors since the end of World War II.[6]

He has seen NATO, the Trans-Pacific Partnership (TPP), and the North American Free Trade Agreement (NAFTA) as commercial arrangements instead of the foundations of an international order led by the United States. He has made decisions that deeply affect the United States' closest partners around the world without consulting them. He has triggered trade dispute after trade dispute. Under his leadership, the United States is more unpopular with publics in many democratic countries than it has been at any time since such polling began in 2001.[7] Indeed, according to the Pew Research Center, more people around the world perceive the United States' "power and influence" to be a "major threat" than they do China's or Russia's.[8]

These statements by the president would surely disturb his predecessors since 1945, from Harry S. Truman to Barack Obama; consider what the soldier-statesman George Marshall would have thought of all this. But for Trump, such destructive remarks are his general style of communication.

With a record like this, much of the U.S. media and national security elite can say little that is good about the president or his foreign policy. Pundits on talk shows, on editorial pages, and in books draw up comprehensive bills of indictment, and rebuttals are infrequent except from the president's most ardent admirers.[9] Many critics condemn most if not all of the president's actions as misguided and driven only, as they see it, by his flawed character, enormous ego, and skewed view of the world.[10] *Foreign Policy* carried a headline that he is "getting away with foreign policy insanity."[11] *USA Today*'s editorial board said there is "no method to his apparent madness."[12] And the editorial board of the *New York Times* asserted that "under Mr. Trump, America surrenders."[13] None of these assertions are models of responsible American journalism, but they do reveal the media's feverish temperature on the subject of Trump's foreign policies.

These critics show no sympathy for the manifold challenges the president faces in trying to deal with a deteriorating world order that he inherited.[14] China rises in disagreeable ways. Europe withdraws, for the first time in five centuries, from a leadership role in global affairs. Russia revives and destabilizes countries in Eastern Europe and beyond. NATO debates its role. The Middle East revisits ancient enmities and generates newer hatreds. India equivocates regarding its global responsibilities. Terrorists murder innocents in much of the world. Global governance falls short. Autocrats successfully disparage democratic values. Technology outstrips nations' and the international system's capabilities to manage it.[15] The United States hesitates, in perceived retreat. Every major country on earth fits T. S. Eliot's description: "But no longer at ease here, in the old dispensation."[16] Not a single U.S. politician has a coherent and convincing set of policies to cope with this eroding world order, but Trump receives nearly all the slings and arrows.

A related question is whether President Trump has a grand strategy. International relations scholars Hal Brands and Colin Kahl define grand strategy as "the conceptual architecture that lends structure and form to foreign policy. A leader who is 'doing grand strategy' is not handling global events on an ad hoc or case-by-case basis. A grand strategy, rather, represents a more purposeful and deeply held set of concepts about a country's goals and orientation in international affairs."[17] At two-plus years into his presidency, does Trump have such a grand strategy that he has been systematically applying to a problematic international environment?

On the face of it, this seems like an odd question. After all, Trump is a president who believes he excels in meetings because he comes unprepared, which he thinks liberates his cunning and creativity.[18] This is a president who lurches from one policy position to another on the same issue, like a spinning top. This is a president who has difficulty discerning policy fact from policy fiction. This is a president who identifies "radical Islamic terrorism" as an existential threat to the United States, but then presses for total U.S. troop withdrawals from Afghanistan and Syria, hotbeds of Islamist terrorists. This is a president who is fixated on unfair trade deals that he argues have been badly negotiated by his predecessors, but then accepts minor changes in the agreements and calls them outstanding. This is a president who thinks NATO is "obsolete," but then builds its defenses. This is a president who sees no danger from Russia, but then fortifies Ukraine. This is a president who asserts that North Korea is a deadly threat to the United States, but then says it is not, despite no consequential change in the situation. This is a president who says he wants to reduce America's overseas commitments, but then threatens to invade Venezuela. These head-spinning dichotomies are not the characteristics of a grand strategist.[19] They appear more like a large bowl of spaghetti bolognese dumped and spread on a white canvas, which some distinguished critics might then stretch to call "an exquisite painterly composition" or, in Trump's case, "a grand strategy." Others might more simply describe the result as "transactional." Call it what you will, it remains a large bowl of spaghetti bolognese dumped and spread on a white canvas.[20]

Nevertheless, in judging all these presidential deficiencies, history teaches us that flawed individuals and policy processes sometimes produce successful results—George Patton's extraordinary victories in France and North Africa come to mind, before his F-grade malfunctions of character caught up with him. Richard M. Nixon was changing world order for the better while he was undermining the American Constitution. As historian Robert Caro describes in some detail, Lyndon B. Johnson was an egocentric, cruel human being, but he managed congressional passage of the 1964 Civil Rights Act and signed significant social spending programs.[21]

Regarding President Trump's lack of interagency coordination, it is also worth remembering that Henry Kissinger choreographed two strategic breakthroughs—the opening to China and détente with the Soviet Union—with little or no formal relevant interagency process. He and Nixon undertook those historic accomplishments from the White House, often without the knowledge of Nixon's national security cabinet members, and would have received an F from them and others on that score.

The estimable Franklin D. Roosevelt made a grievous and unsuccessful F attempt to pack the Supreme Court in 1937, and George W. Bush ordered the disastrous 2003 invasion of Iraq, a historic F decision. (History gives no credit for good intentions.) In addition, aggressively confronting allies who act in ways that damage U.S. national interests is not a mortal sin, as Dwight D. Eisenhower made clear to the British and French governments during the 1956 Suez Crisis. London and Paris without question gave President Eisenhower an F for alliance solidarity.

In assessing all these episodes, what matters most is the effectiveness of U.S. policy over time and its consistency with U.S. national interests, not the personal qualities of its leaders.

The nearly universal condemnation of the president's foreign policies is also fed by his process of making and announcing decisions and his execution of them, from countless tweets, to changing policy goals, to his explanations of policy that differ from those of his senior advisors. But this automatic dismissal of President Trump's foreign policy is too simple. It lacks a careful examination of Trump's and his administration's objectives, strategies, and policies; their connections to U.S. national interests; or their actual successes and failures.[22]

This Council Special Report takes a different approach. It examines in detail Trump's actions in a turbulent world in important policy areas, including the United States' relationships with its allies, its relationships with China and Russia, and its policies on the Middle East and climate change. This report acknowledges the persuasive points of Trump's critics, but at the same time seeks to perform exacting autopsies on their less convincing critiques. It then gives a grade to each of the president's major foreign policies. (Other issues could have been included, such as policies toward Africa, AIDS, and pandemics, but those addressed in this report will likely dominate history's judgment of the president's foreign policies.)

Finally, this report comes to a net assessment of the overall quality of the Trump administration's foreign policy halfway through his first term.

Some could argue that grading the president is a crude way to measure his foreign policy, that it inevitably misses nuance and complexity. Such a yardstick certainly has its limitations. However, Trump assesses his own performance in this way. In an interview with Chris Wallace on Fox News, President Trump compared his job performance with that of past presidents and said, "I would give myself an A+," perhaps based on his own view that he is a "very stable genius."[23] (Not everyone agrees with the president. In a January 2019 *Politico/Morning Consult* poll, 42 percent of respondents gave the president either a D or an F on foreign policy.[24]) Recognizing the inherent shortcomings of this approach, this report adopts the president's own metric in evaluating his policies.

However, this approach raises a serious methodological issue: whether Trump's grades should be based on his success or failure in carrying out his policy objectives, whatever their merits, or on whether his policies, notwithstanding his goals, promote U.S. national interests.[25] The first possibility is challenging to apply for three reasons. First, Trump's policy objectives and his strategies to accomplish them are often unclear. (For example, it is unknown what his policy intentions are vis-à-vis the U.S. role in defending Europe.[26] It is also unknown what his strategy is to coerce Tehran to forgo the option of acquiring nuclear weapons, and whether it includes going to war against Iran.) Second, there are frequent gaps between the president's policy instincts and goals and those of his major national security advisors, as is shown in the cases of Afghanistan, Russia, Syria, and perhaps China. (The president is fixated on Beijing's predatory trade practices, but it is unclear that he shares his administration's broader concerns about the dangerous geopolitical implications of the rise and application of Chinese power.) Third, if Trump achieves a foreign policy objective through diligence and determination that undermines America's national interests—as in cozying up to Putin's Russia or weakening progress on climate change—this approach would assign him a passing grade, despite the problematic results.

While attempting to understand the president's policy goals, this report takes the second approach and grades the president on whether his policies promote U.S. national interests. These judgments, and therefore Trump's grades in this report, are thus inevitably based in part on preconceived notions of what ought to be the pillars of U.S. national interests, foreign policy, and statecraft.

# CHINA

U.S. foreign policies toward another nation rarely succeed if policymakers do not conduct careful studies of that country's national security goals and strategies. Careless or inadequate analysis can have damaging or even catastrophic consequences. British governments misunderstood Adolf Hitler's intentions in the 1930s. The Johnson administration in the 1960s was blind to North Vietnam's determination, staying power, and refusal to give up any of its strategic objectives. Before the 2003 invasion, the George W. Bush team knew too little about the dysfunctional political and ethnic dynamics of Iraq, and ignored Baghdad's indispensable role in balancing Tehran. History is filled with such miscalculations, going back to the Romans, the Greeks, the Egyptians, the Chinese, and earlier.[27]

Long before Trump took office, successive U.S. administrations pursued approaches to China that misread Beijing's strategic intentions. A 1997 statement issued at the Bill Clinton-Jiang Zemin summit observed that "while China and the United States have areas of both agreement and disagreement, they have a significant common interest and a firm common will to seize opportunities and meet challenges cooperatively, with candor and a determination to achieve concrete progress," and that "the two Presidents are determined to build toward a constructive strategic partnership between China and the United States through increasing cooperation to meet international challenges and promote peace and development in the world."[28]

At a 2001 joint press conference with Jiang Zemin, George W. Bush said that "today's meetings convinced me that we can build on our common interests. . . . We seek a relationship that is candid, constructive, and cooperative."[29]

In a joint press conference with Xi Jinping in 2015, Barack Obama noted that "as a result of our efforts, our two nations are working together more closely across a broader range of critical issues—and our cooperation is delivering results, for both our nations and the world."[30]

While these presidents were making such optimistic statements over a nearly twenty-year period, China implemented a grand strategy designed to undermine U.S.-Asian alliances, which has accelerated under Xi Jinping; used geoeconomic tools to coerce its neighbors and others, including most recently through the Belt and Road Initiative (BRI); violated international commercial practices, including by committing massive theft of U.S. intellectual property; manipulated its currency for trade benefits; threatened Taiwan; built up its military forces to push the United States beyond Japan and the Philippines; constructed and militarized artificial islands in the South China Sea, in violation of international law; systemically and brutally violated the human rights of its own people; and patiently and incrementally built its power and influence with the strategic goal of replacing the United States as the primary power in Asia.[31]

As former Singaporean Prime Minister Lee Kuan Yew put it, China has "a culture 4,000 years old with 1.3 billion people, many of great talent.... How could they not aspire to be number 1 in Asia, and in time the world?"[32] Not recognizing the clarity of Lee's conclusion, successive administrations spoke routinely about their "engage and hedge" strategy against Chinese misbehavior, long after Beijing had seriously misbehaved and when that hedging should have changed into something much stronger and more decisive to counter China's threats to U.S. vital national interests.

These American misunderstandings of China's objectives over nearly two decades rank as one of the three most damaging U.S. foreign policy errors since the end of World War II, along with the 1965 military escalation in Vietnam and the 2003 invasion of Iraq. Indeed, this prolonged failure in China policy could turn out to be the biggest U.S. policy deficiency in the past seven decades, given the accumulating dangerous strategic consequences of the rise of Chinese power for world order as well as for the United States and its allies and friends.

It was not inevitable that the U.S.-China relationship would evolve into its current adversarial standoff. If Washington, through careful and consistent diplomacy in coordination with its Asian allies, had routinely contested Beijing's aggressive policies much earlier, China, then weaker, could have pulled back and a rough equilibrium could have been established and maintained, with major areas of cooperation. And if Beijing instead had continued on that confrontational path, the United States would have been in a stronger position to respond than it is at present. But the Chinese leadership, faced with successively acquiescent U.S. administrations that miscalculated China's strategic intentions, went on pushing until it finally provoked a Thermidorean reaction from the United States.[33]

President Trump got off to a terrible start in managing the U.S.-China relationship by withdrawing from the TPP on January 23, 2017. The twelve-nation agreement (Australia, Brunei, Canada, Chile, Japan, Malaysia, Mexico, New Zealand, Peru, Singapore, Vietnam, and the United States) would have reduced tariff and nontariff barriers to U.S. exports to Asian markets. The TPP was the most important U.S. geoeconomic response to the increasingly coercive weight of the Chinese economy in Asia. It offered Asian nations trade alternatives to their dependence on China, which often brought with it Chinese geopolitical pressure. President Trump killed it with no serious analysis of the TPP's significant geoeconomic and geopolitical benefits for the United States.[34]

To its credit, however, the Trump administration has since adopted a much more clear-eyed approach regarding China that breaks with many of the errors of the past. The administration did an about-face after exiting the TPP that was reflected in its December 2017 National Security Strategy. That document stressed that "China is using economic inducements and penalties, influence operations, and implied military threats to persuade other states to heed its political and security agenda," and that China is expanding its influence in Africa, Europe, South Asia, and the Western Hemisphere while stealing "hundreds of billions" of dollars' worth of American intellectual property.[35]

Similarly, the January 2018 National Defense Strategy judged that "China is a strategic competitor using predatory economics to intimidate its neighbors while militarizing features in the South China Sea."[36] And on October 4, 2018, Vice President Mike Pence delivered the toughest speech on U.S.-China relations by a U.S. administration in fifty years, stressing that

> China now spends as much on its military as the rest of Asia combined, and Beijing has prioritized capabilities to erode America's military advantages on land, at sea, in the air, and in space. China wants nothing less than to push the United States of America from the Western Pacific and attempt to prevent us from coming to the aid of our allies.[37]

The administration also recognizes that Beijing's efforts to develop emerging technologies could put the United States at a competitive disadvantage. On February 11, 2019, President Trump signed the American AI Initiative executive order, which is designed to "promote sustained investment in AI [artificial intelligence] R&D in collaboration with industry, academia, international partners and allies, and other non-Federal entities," to "reduce barriers to the use of AI technologies to promote their innovative application," and to "train the next generation of American AI researchers and users through apprenticeships; skills programs; and education in science, technology, engineering, and mathematics."[38]

At the same time, the administration backed up its rhetoric with action, although Trump is more narrowly focused on trade and it is unclear how much he has internalized his administration's broader containment policy regarding China. The president publicly and loudly confronted Beijing and its long-standing unfair trade practices. Most notably, the administration imposed tariffs on $250 billion in Chinese imports to the United States with the goal of forcing China to open market access to U.S. firms, ending forced technology transfers to Chinese firms, and curbing subsidies to state-owned industries.[39] The United States threatened to raise rates on March 2, 2019, if no deal was reached, but later extended the deadline after reporting it was making "substantial progress" in trade negotiations.[40] Despite having such a fundamental misunderstanding of the dynamics of international commerce and the role of trade deficits and tariffs, as highlighted below, Trump has succeeded in cleverly pressing China.[41]

The president's confrontational trade policy could lead to a significant deal. How negotiations will turn out is unclear at this writing, but press reports indicate that Trump could receive serious trade

concessions from the Chinese government that his immediate predecessors sought but could not get through diplomatic entreaties.[42]
(Making progress on China's theft of U.S. intellectual property is a
much harder problem.[43]) It remains possible that Beijing will yet again
not make good on its commitments, but Trump and his often-criticized
trade strategy could have broken through Beijing's heretofore impene-
trable shield regarding its trade misconduct.

The Trump administration has taken further actions against individual Chinese firms, though these have been inconsistent. Based
on charges that Chinese telecom firm Huawei had evaded sanctions
against Iran and on fears that its entry into 5G networks could allow
China to gain even greater access to commercial secrets and classified
government information, the United States persuaded Canadian police
to arrest Chief Financial Officer Meng Wanzhou, formally charged the
company with fraud, and pressured allies to not allow Huawei to work
on 5G networks within their borders.[44] The United States reportedly
intends to follow up with an executive order preventing Chinese firms
from building new networks in the United States.[45] Chinese telecom
firm ZTE also violated Iran sanctions, but the president lifted an existing U.S. ban on doing business with the company as part of an effort to
open up market access in China.[46]

On balance, however, the president has placed more economic
pressure on Beijing to change its trade practices than did any of his predecessors since China began its remarkable economic growth in the
1990s. This is all to the good.

Sometimes continuing policies initiated by President Obama, the
Trump administration has similarly worked to push back against China's growing influence on regional security in Asia and has sought to
improve the United States' ability to project power into the region.
The number of deployable U.S. Navy ships across the entire fleet has
increased from 273 in December 2016, right before President Trump
took office, to 287 in January 2019.[47] In the South China Sea, which
China claims as its territory in violation of international law, the navy
has conducted at least ten freedom of navigation operations during
the Trump administration. By February 2019, these amounted to more
than twice as many as the Obama administration conducted in its eight
years.[48] (The Chinese government has stated that it believes these
operations "infringed upon Chinese sovereignty, and undermined the
peace, security, and order of the relevant waters."[49]) The Trump administration remains determined to keep a strong U.S. presence in contested spaces in the western Pacific.

These efforts to strengthen the U.S. military's deployments in Asia are not limited to the U.S. Navy. Noting the importance of combat aircraft for missions over large distances in the western Pacific and Indian Oceans, U.S. Indo-Pacific Command (INDOPACOM) has prioritized placing the most advanced warplanes in forward positions, including the F-35 and the P-8 Poseidon maritime patrol plane and many unmanned aerial vehicles (UAVs), in addition to its already deployed long-range bombers.[50] The Pentagon is funding the research and development of UAVs and other unmanned systems, along with long-range anti-ship missiles, to compensate for surface ships' increasing vulnerability to anti-access/area denial tools like land-based missile attacks.[51]

INDOPACOM has also sought to make its supply networks and bases more resilient, in response to China's greater capability to deliver concentrated attacks against specific targets using long-range missiles. The defense posture realignment initiative, begun during the Obama administration and continuing today, has involved new construction to relocate some bases that were previously concentrated in Guam and Okinawa to new areas around the Pacific Rim, in addition to reinforcing the construction of existing facilities. In the same vein, INDOPACOM has started efforts to "disaggregate" its supply stockpiles and to improve its ability to communicate with regional allies in the event of a conflict.[52]

Despite the president's erratic stances on trade, the Trump administration has maintained robust relationships at multiple levels with Japan and other traditional regional partners. INDOPACOM has carried out increased military exercises with the Japan Self-Defense Forces, including the annual Keen Sword air and sea exercise, which involved fifty-seven thousand troops in 2018.[53] In December 2018, Tokyo announced plans to spend $10 billion on 147 F-35 jets, making it the largest non-U.S. buyer of the aircraft.[54] Japan has also provided essential support for U.S. efforts to disperse U.S. bases across its territories. And the United States and Australia conducted their largest exercise ever, with thirty-three thousand total personnel taking part in Talisman Saber 2017.[55]

U.S. support for militaries in the Asia-Pacific does not apply only to treaty allies. The Trump administration has worked to make India a more prominent part of its regional strategy (discussed below). After changing the name of U.S. Pacific Command to U.S. Indo-Pacific Command in May 2018, the United States is now planning its first tri-service exercise with the Indian military.[56] In addition to maintaining the Obama administration's Southeast Asia Maritime Security Initiative (renaming it the Indo-Pacific Maritime Security Initiative), which was designed to improve the capacity of U.S. allies and partners to respond to regional threats, the Trump administration provided an additional $300 million to countries in Southeast Asia for improving communications systems and patrol capabilities around the Bay of Bengal, the South China Sea, and many Pacific islands.[57]

The administration has also taken steps to craft and implement a geoeconomic response to China's BRI to provide an alternative to, as Vice President Pence put it, "a constricting belt [and] a one-way road."[58] China uses the debts that BRI recipients incur to take possession of strategic assets such as ports and energy infrastructure across Asia and beyond.[59] Even though more and more countries have recognized Beijing's partly malign intentions with the initiative, some still accept the funding, and the size of China's efforts has far exceeded offerings from other sources.[60] Washington has begun some of its own development programs across the region, including $25 million for telecommunications projects, $50 million for energy infrastructure, and $30 million for a new Infrastructure Transaction and Assistance Network to coordinate funding, although these are pitifully small numbers compared to BRI; estimates of its size range from $25 billion to $300 billion.[61] The United States' Overseas Private Investment Corporation (OPIC) already has $3.9 billion invested in the Indo-Pacific, and its successor organization, the U.S. International Development Finance Corporation, will have more than double OPIC's lending authority, creating more openings for new projects.[62] The administration also announced that it would work with Australia and Japan to provide increased alternatives to Chinese investment.[63] But Washington will have to promote massive amounts of additional private investment if it hopes to successfully counter Beijing's efforts to use geoeconomic coercion to achieve its regional and global geopolitical goals.[64] This is where the U.S. withdrawal from the TPP especially hurts.

Even as it implements these policies to deal with the threatening aspects of the rise of Chinese power, the Trump administration has failed to construct a plausible path of classic diplomacy with Beijing that would ameliorate the growing tension between the two countries.[65] A supreme effort by both sides is necessary to avoid a situation of permanent confrontation, which could eventually lead to war, in particular over the issue of Taiwan, where tensions between Beijing and Taipei are on the rise.[66]

Instead of seeking a sustained strategic dialogue with Beijing, the Trump team publicly issues policy ultimatums to China.[67] Given Beijing's increasing power and influence and the effects of nineteenth-century imperial treaty ports on Chinese psychology, Trump's approach of forswearing traditional diplomatic instruments is unlikely to succeed, even if it could yield some benefits in the trade domain.

If Washington and Beijing do not stop the downward spiral in the bilateral relationship and lurch into prolonged intense confrontation or even conflict, the American and Chinese people would be the first to pay the price of this policy failure.[68] Most of the rest of the world would soon join the suffering. Consequences would emerge for the United States' and China's formidable domestic challenges and national economies. Effects on the global economy would be devastating. Tension would dramatically increase throughout Asia, since no country in that vast region wants to have to choose between the United States and China.[69] The effect on potential U.S.-China collaboration on climate change and other issues of global governance would be corrosive. Attempts to deal with the nuclear weapons program of North Korea and potentially that of Iran would fall apart.

Well-intentioned civil servants will not have the political steam to get this U.S.-China bilateral train moving in the right direction. Both Washington and Beijing will make their positions clear in public pronouncements, but the serious differences between the two sides are unlikely to narrow. Therefore, talks should be modeled after Henry Kissinger's private discussions with Zhou Enlai in the early 1970s. As Kissinger notes in his book *On China*, from 1972 onward, "What we encountered was a diplomatic style closer to traditional Chinese diplomacy than to the pedantic formulations to which we had become accustomed during our negotiations with other Communist states."[70]

In a restricted government-to-government format well away from the public eye, U.S. and Chinese leaders should, first, candidly address how the application of their countries' perceived national interests can be circumscribed and restrained to avoid U.S.-China confrontation. Without this sustained strategic dialogue to discuss what sorts of restraint are required from each side, the future relationship between the United States and China looks exceedingly bleak. Although such extended exchanges at high levels between Washington and Beijing will not end the strategic competition between the two, which will last for decades, they could help avoid worst-case outcomes. At this writing, many doubt that either side at present is capable of mounting a serious strategic dialogue, but what is the alternative to giving it a try? In any case, no such discussion is in the offing from either capital, and the president and his team bear some responsibility for that.

However, for an intensified high-level bilateral dialogue between Washington and Beijing to be fruitful, the United States should first clearly establish that it is enhancing its military, diplomatic, and economic power projection into Asia, intensifying interaction with allies and friends, and helping build up their military strength—not just making speeches about competition. This is especially true regarding Japan, the most important U.S. ally in Asia and the world.[71] Nothing less will convince Beijing that it has reasons, based on its national interests, to negotiate seriously with the United States. This will take some time, for Beijing will wait to see if Washington becomes distracted and diverts its attention to other lesser issues in the daily headlines, as is its wont.

The United States has just entered the fourth phase of its relationship with China since the end of World War II. In phase one, the United States sought and failed to prevent Mao Zedong from taking power, which produced a long period of antagonistic interaction. Phase two saw Richard Nixon and Henry Kissinger open up the relationship to better meet the global Soviet threat and, they thought, to help end the Vietnam War. In phase three, Washington sought to bring Beijing ever more into the international system, hoping it would eventually become a "responsible stakeholder" and accede to U.S.-fashioned rules of the international order.[72] Phase four has just begun, with the United States fully digesting the threatening implications of the rise of Chinese power and taking initial actions to deal with it effectively. It remains to be seen whether the Trump administration and its successors are up to the task of addressing this enormous Chinese challenge in the decades ahead. President Trump and his colleagues do not yet have an enduring and encompassing grand strategy to do so.

All the same, overall the president deserves a high grade for his policies on China. His administration has taken the lead in awakening the United States to the growing threat that China poses to U.S. vital national interests and democratic values. Regarding the latter and in the context of Xi Jinping's internal crackdown, George Soros stressed at the January 2019 Davos conference, "China isn't the only authoritarian regime in the world, but it's undoubtedly the wealthiest, strongest and most developed in machine learning and artificial intelligence. This makes Xi Jinping the most dangerous opponent of those who believe in the concept of open society."[73] Without the Trump administration's persistent political push regarding the increasing dangers of Chinese power, America could well have continued sleepwalking while Beijing decisively drew large parts of Asia into its orbit and away from the United States.

Now the challenge for the president and his successors is to persuade Beijing, through enhanced U.S. power projection, more able alliances, and adroit diplomacy, that the United States will grow ever stronger in Asia and, with its allies and friends, will robustly confront destabilizing Chinese actions. If Xi Jinping and his colleagues could be brought to such a conclusion, Washington and Beijing could then work to create and sustain a new and stable balance of power in Asia and to avoid the catastrophic outcomes that a permanent confrontation between the United States and China is likely to bring. This is the profound diplomatic challenge for the leaderships of both countries over the decades ahead.

*Trump Grade on China Policy: B+*

# CLIMATE CHANGE

Almost all world leaders other than Trump accept that the actions of humans contribute to climate change and the warming of the planet. From 2012 onward, the president has made statements including "The concept of global warming was created by and for the Chinese in order to make U.S. manufacturing non-competitive"; "We should be focused on magnificently clean and healthy air and not distracted by the expensive hoax that is global warming!"; "Give me clean, beautiful and healthy air - not the same old climate change (global warming) bullshit! I am tired of hearing this nonsense"; and "I don't see" the climate change effects warned about in a 1,600-page National Climate Assessment released by his own administration.[74] During an especially cold period in early 2019, he tweeted, "What the hell is going on with Global Waming [sic]? Please come back fast, we need you!"[75] In his February 2019 State of the Union speech, which lasted eighty-two minutes and was the third longest in history, he did not mention climate change.[76]

It is unnecessary to include extensive rebuttals to Trump's remarks regarding climate change, because such evidence is well known and undeniable.[77] The president's views on this subject led him to announce on June 1, 2017, that the United States would withdraw from the Paris Agreement. Trump argued that the accord, which was created to get the world to commit to lowering carbon emissions, would put the United States "at a permanent disadvantage."[78] Undercutting the concept of global climate governance, the Trump administration's withdrawal will make it difficult to reach even the minimum Paris Agreement target of preventing global temperatures from rising more than 2°C.[79]

Although China generates approximately 28 percent of global carbon emissions and the United States is responsible for only about 15 percent, the U.S. withdrawal from the Paris Agreement has made China an informal global leader on climate change, as the signatories of the agreement proceed without U.S. involvement.[80] This contributes to a widespread international view that the United States, reflected in the policies of the Trump administration, is withdrawing from the world.[81] Many U.S. global business leaders were against President Trump's decision.[82] Moreover, his actions will not save U.S. coal production, as he argued. While coal exports saw a 61 percent increase in 2017, coal production fell in 2018 and is expected to decline further as the United States makes advances in natural gas extraction and renewable energy technology.[83]

Despite Trump's denials, climate change is increasingly weakening the national security of the United States. Although the president does not believe in climate change, the Pentagon does. In a 2019 report, the Department of Defense found that "climate-related events," including "recurrent flooding, drought, desertification, wildfires, and thawing permafrost," either caused damage or had the potential to damage seventy-nine U.S. military installations around the world.[84] The report further noted that climate-related issues not only affect the military's ability to react to crises and force the Department of Defense to devote more resources to repairing facilities and equipment, but also create weather conditions that make operations more difficult in Africa, the Arctic, Europe, and elsewhere.[85] Former U.S. Secretary of Defense Jim Mattis similarly warned shortly after his confirmation hearings that "climate change is impacting stability in areas of the world where our troops are operating today. . . . It is appropriate for the Combatant Commands to incorporate drivers of instability that impact the security environment in their areas into their planning."[86]

The U.S. intelligence community, too, believes that global climate change is a significant threat to U.S. national interests. In a February

2018 report to Congress, Director of National Intelligence Daniel Coats noted that the rapid changes to global climate systems would "raise the risk of humanitarian disasters, conflict, water and food shortages, population migration, labor shortfalls, price shocks, and power outages," and that "worsening air pollution from forest burning, agricultural waste incineration, urbanization, and rapid industrialization—with increasing public awareness—might drive protests against authorities, such as those recently in China, India, and Iran."[87] These intelligence agencies concluded that "the impacts of the long-term trends toward a warming climate, more air pollution, biodiversity loss, and water scarcity are likely to fuel economic and social discontent—and possibly upheaval—through 2018" and beyond.[88] The January 2019 report maintained this conclusion, observing that "extreme weather, higher temperatures, droughts, floods, wildfires, storms, sea level rise, soil degradation, and acidifying oceans are intensifying, threatening infrastructure, health, and water and food security."[89] Yet in February 2019, when the Trump administration proposed to assemble a panel of people to discuss climate change's effects on U.S. security, it sought to include at least one White House staffer who does not believe that carbon emissions have caused environmental problems.[90]

Climate change is undeniably a serious threat to U.S. national security and to the country's way of life, yet the president's rhetoric and policies exacerbate rather than combat the problem. As Michael Brune of the Sierra Club said, the withdrawal from the Paris accord was a "historic mistake which our grandchildren will look back on with stunned dismay at how a world leader could be so divorced from reality and morality."[91] This may be one of the few times the Pentagon and the Sierra Club have aligned on a policy issue.

It is difficult to know what is driving President Trump's climate policies at home and abroad, other than pure ignorance. But if his objective is to undermine concerted international efforts regarding climate and to weaken the U.S. government's policies to address climate change within the United States, unfortunately he is succeeding. This policy "success" does not give him a passing grade.

*Trump Grade on Climate Change Policy: F*

# NORTH KOREA

Upon assuming office, Trump inherited a dismal situation with respect to the nuclear weapons held by the Democratic People's Republic of Korea (DPRK), not least because of the failed policies of his immediate three predecessors.[92] Although previous administrations tried again and again to coerce Pyongyang to give up its nuclear weapons or to negotiate that outcome, North Korea went on expanding its nuclear arsenal and developing ever longer-range ballistic missiles.[93]

In 1993, North Korea announced plans to exit the Nuclear Nonproliferation Treaty (NPT) and began to enrich plutonium at its Yongbyon reactor.[94] After seriously considering military action against North Korea, the Clinton administration chose to negotiate, and it finalized the U.S.-DPRK Agreed Framework in October 1994. Under the agreement, Pyongyang temporarily stopped its activities at Yongbyon in exchange for U.S. support to build two light-water nuclear reactors (which could not be used to enrich plutonium). The United States would provide fuel oil while those reactors were being constructed.[95]

However, North Korea proliferated missile and nuclear technology to Iran, Pakistan, and Syria, and in 1998 North Korea began to test three-stage rockets in an attempt to build its long-range ballistic missile capability, provoking another crisis and more negotiations.[96] Thus Clinton passed on a failed policy to his successor.

When the George W. Bush administration entered office, it believed that negotiations were the least bad option, but the U.S. intelligence community found that North Korea had sought an alternative path to a nuclear weapon through highly enriched uranium, which it did not need the Yongbyon facilities to produce.[97] President Bush, perhaps taking into account Deputy Secretary of Defense Paul Wolfowitz's assessment that the North Korean regime was "teetering on the edge of economic collapse," abrogated the Agreed Framework and reimposed sanctions on Pyongyang.[98] North Korea was listed, with Iran and Iraq, as a member of the "axis of evil."[99]

With the Agreed Framework no longer in place, Pyongyang formally withdrew from the NPT in January 2003, restarted the Yongbyon reactor, and began to produce plutonium there again. The Bush team, which was focused on making a case for war in Iraq, in 2003 began the Six Party Talks with China, Japan, North Korea, Russia, and South Korea in an attempt to persuade North Korea to stop its nuclear weapons programs. As the talks dragged on, President Bush increased sanctions, and in September 2005 he threatened penalties on Macau's Banco Delta Asia, which laundered the Kim Jong-il regime's money so it could evade sanctions. This threat dramatically reduced Banco Delta Asia's revenue and prompted the bank to freeze North Korean accounts; the Bank of China's Macau branch, fearing expanded sanctions, also blocked Pyongyang's access to funds. North Korea promptly left the Six Party Talks.[100]

In October 2006, North Korea successfully detonated a nuclear device. Afterward, Bush lifted the Banco Delta Asia sanctions and sought to restart the Six Party Talks. The Bush team proposed to remove North Korea's designation as a state sponsor of terrorism and to send $400 million in food and fuel if North Korea shut down Yongbyon.[101] Pyongyang did temporarily close the facility, but it maintained its nuclear arsenal and also sent nuclear technology to Syria, which the Israeli Air Force destroyed in 2007.[102] President Bush continued to negotiate despite these North Korean violations and passed on a failed policy to his successor.

Shortly after Barack Obama became president, North Korea conducted a ballistic missile test and the United Nations increased sanctions. Pyongyang ended its participation in the Six Party Talks, reopened Yongbyon, and conducted additional nuclear and missile tests.[103] The Obama administration did not pursue new talks and instead adopted a policy of "strategic patience": it increased sanctions and cyber operations to slow North Korea's nuclear progress, with the idea that the increased pressure would force Pyongyang to come back to the negotiating table and give up, or at least constrain, its nuclear program.[104]

In December 2011 the leader of North Korea, Kim Jong-il, died, and his son Kim Jong-un succeeded him. In February 2012 the Obama administration, hoping the new leader would be open to reform, concluded the Leap Day Deal with North Korea: Pyongyang would halt its missile tests, nuclear tests, and Yongbyon activity in exchange for significant food aid. At the time, North Korea accepted the terms, but it soon violated the accord, testing missiles in April and December 2012 and a nuclear weapon in February 2013.[105] The Obama administration persisted in the policy of strategic patience, hoping it could prevent North Korea from developing a nuclear-armed intercontinental ballistic missile (ICBM) that could strike the continental United States. Meanwhile, Pyongyang increased the number of its nuclear weapons, now estimated to be between twenty and sixty, and worked to extend the range of its ballistic missiles.[106] Thus Obama, too, passed on a failed policy to his successor.

When Trump won the election, Obama allegedly briefed him that North Korea was the most pressing issue he would need to address as president.[107] Pyongyang could not yet strike the U.S. mainland with a nuclear weapon delivered by a ballistic missile, but it was rapidly building its capabilities to reach that objective. In March 2017, Kim sent four ballistic missiles near the Chinese border on an upward trajectory; they landed within Japan's exclusive economic zone.[108] After testing an ICBM to coincide with the anniversary of the cease-fire of the Korean War, Pyongyang launched another ballistic missile on July 28, 2017, that theoretically would have been able to reach the continental United States if placed on a flatter trajectory.[109] On August 5, 2017, as a result of the Trump administration's urging, the UN Security Council unanimously adopted a U.S.-sponsored resolution to tighten sanctions against North Korea.[110]

In response to these new sanctions, North Korean state media announced that it would seek "thousands-fold revenge" on the United States.[111] On August 8, 2017, President Trump responded, "North Korea best not make any more threats to the United States. They will be met with fire and fury like the world has never seen."[112] This statement was widely criticized at the time, but it is worth asking what would have been an appropriate reaction from the president.[113] For twenty-five years, presidents had tried negotiations, economic pressure, and repeated admonitions to slow the North Korean nuclear program. All failed. Those carefully worded, antiseptic approaches led to nothing except an ever more dangerous North Korea. Instead, as is his wont, Trump dramatically raised the stakes and shook up everyone's expectations. North Korea continued to conduct missile tests, including two flight tests that sent missiles over Japan.[114] On September 3, 2017, it released a photograph of what appeared to be a miniaturized nuclear weapon shortly before its sixth nuclear test.[115]

The president's critics charge that he initiated this crisis with North Korea, only to take credit for solving it. This was not the case. The latest confrontation between North Korea and the United States was a result of Pyongyang's testing of nuclear weapons and ballistic missiles, as well as explicit North Korean threats against the United States, to which Trump responded in his own way.

In a speech to the UN General Assembly on September 19, 2017, President Trump stressed that if the United States or its allies were attacked, the United States would "have no choice but to totally destroy North Korea," adding, "Rocket Man is on a suicide mission for himself and for his regime."[116] On December 22, the UN Security Council, with China voting in favor, passed even tougher North Korea sanctions, which heavily restricted fuel imports and required countries that employed North Korean workers to send them back.[117] Nevertheless, on January 1, 2018, Kim declared that his nuclear arsenal was "capable of thwarting and countering any nuclear threats from the United States."[118]

But in March 2018, when Kim surprised the world by offering to meet with Trump and discuss nuclear issues, Trump accepted on the spot.[119] Kim presumably would not have proposed a summit meeting had Trump not escalated the crisis and thus disrupted the unsatisfactory status quo. Although Trump threatened to cancel the meeting after North Korea called Vice President Pence "ignorant and stupid" for warning that Kim could end up like Muammar al-Qaddafi, the summit occurred as planned on June 12, 2018, in Singapore.[120] The two leaders stated that "President Trump committed to provide security guarantees to the DPRK, and Chairman Kim Jong-un reaffirmed his firm and unwavering commitment to complete denuclearization of the Korean Peninsula."[121] However, despite Trump's assertions that "there is no longer a nuclear threat from North Korea," Kim did not commit to a specific denuclearization program or timetable.[122]

President Trump also decided at that summit meeting that "war games" with South Korea should be suspended. Although Seoul was reportedly not consulted in advance of this concession, such exercises did not take place in August and October.[123] Trump also demanded that South Korea pay the United States more for its troops stationed on the Korean Peninsula, only to claim that South Korea increased its contributions far more than it actually did, confusing allies, adversaries, and U.S. officials.[124] The Trump administration has also failed to manage rising tensions between Japan and South Korea over disagreements about how to address Japanese atrocities committed during World War II and territorial disputes over islands; this lack of a united front could make the U.S. strategy more difficult to execute.[125] (Trump has insulted Japan, too; during his presidential campaign, he stated that if the United States were attacked, the Japanese "can sit at home and watch Sony television."[126])

After the summit, Kim repatriated the remains of fifty-five U.S. soldiers and began to dismantle a missile launch site.[127] The Trump administration maintains that "final, fully verified denuclearization" is necessary for sanctions to be lifted, but North Korea demands U.S. guarantees of security before giving up any of its nuclear weapons.[128] The Singapore summit declaration did not directly address this sequencing issue.

The sanctions regime on North Korea has weakened since the meeting in Singapore, and in July 2018 China and Russia blocked U.S.-led efforts in the United Nations to investigate sanctions compliance by Pyongyang.[129] In October 2018, Secretary of State Mike Pompeo met with Kim and set the groundwork for a second Trump-Kim meeting, which occurred in Hanoi, Vietnam, on February 27 and 28, 2019.[130]

In November 2018, the *New York Times* broke the story that North Korea had only partially dismantled the missile launch site, started improvement projects at more than twelve others, and produced more missiles and fissile material.[131] North Korea also claimed that it had tested an "ultramodern tactical weapon" that month, though it was not clear what that meant.[132] Nevertheless, U.S. Special Representative for North Korea Stephen Biegun announced in a January 31, 2019, speech that North Korea promised to destroy all its facilities for making fuel for nuclear bombs.[133] The relevant word is "promised."

Contrary to what much of the media reported and many pundits opined, the late-February Trump-Kim summit in Hanoi did not "collapse," nor was it a "humiliation" for the president.[134] These are further examples of instinctive bias against Trump. Rather, like many summits before it, after tough talks it did not end in accord between the two parties because differences could not be reconciled.[135] Although Trump seemed to place too much confidence in his personal ability to sway Kim, and complex negotiations between leaders is not the ideal way to reach agreement, Trump rightly refused to accept the North Korean offer to dismantle the Yongbyon nuclear weapons facility (three square miles and three hundred buildings) in return for the United States' lifting all sanctions against Pyongyang.[136]

This offer to dismantle Yongbyon was vague and would also have left North Korea with all its intercontinental missiles, all the weapons-grade plutonium already produced, and all the nuclear devices it has stored; allowed the continued production of nuclear weapons; kept its entire nuclear inventory secret; and not disclosed its secret facilities to enrich uranium and perhaps plutonium.[137] As Susan Rice, Obama's former national security advisor, put it, "For the United States to have agreed to lift all sanctions in the absence of real and complete denuclearization would have been a tremendous mistake."[138]

Where the Trump-Kim exchanges go from here is unclear, although North Korea apparently began rebuilding major missile-test facilities immediately after the Hanoi summit.[139] If Pyongyang tests a ballistic missile, a fundamental reevaluation of U.S. policy toward North Korea will obviously be required. North Korea is highly unlikely to give up its nuclear arsenal, which is the surest guarantee of the continuation of the regime. Washington should finally come to this conclusion and concentrate on an urgent effort to trade some North Korean restraint in its nuclear weapons and missile programs for some relief in sanctions. In addition, the president should not make any more unilateral concessions, as he did when he permanently canceled U.S.-South Korean major military exercises.

Trump's strategy at this writing has calmed the situation and reinvigorated the negotiating track by having U.S. and North Korean officials meet at the highest level for the first time in history.[140] He has addressed, at least temporarily, what matters most to U.S. vital national interests—the suspension of North Korea's nuclear and missile tests, whose systems directly threaten the U.S. mainland. It appears unlikely that this would have happened without Trump's dramatic if unorthodox approach, and through his negotiation the United States is now in a somewhat better position to reduce the threat from North Korean nuclear weapons and ballistic missiles than it was when he entered office. At a minimum, he has delayed the moment when a U.S. president would have to either stand by while North Korea progressively expanded its nuclear weapon and ballistic missile capabilities, or attack its nuclear and missile sites, which could lead to a nuclear war on the Korean Peninsula and beyond.

*Trump Grade on North Korea Policy: B*

# NATO AND EUROPEAN SECURITY

President Trump's policy objectives regarding U.S.-European relations remain obscure. He might wish to engineer a new and vigorous balance of effort within the alliance to bolster NATO's defense and deterrence, or he might seek to incrementally weaken U.S. commitments to and involvement in the defense of Europe. Among allied governments and publics, he is raising doubts regarding the United States' commitment to NATO.

The president's never-ending hostility toward these transatlantic allies, however, is not the most striking dimension of Europe today.[141] Rather, it is Europe's withdrawal from global geopolitics for the first time since the sixteenth century and the beginning of the age of European colonialism.[142] Preoccupied with the disparate innards of the European Union, sluggish economies, and antidemocratic trends, European governments are nearly nowhere to be seen in addressing the troubling dimensions of the rise of China, including its coercive geo-economic policies and its pernicious influence on global governance; the eroding balance of power in Asia; the Shia-Sunni power struggle in the Middle East and Iran's hegemonic ambitions in the region; the expansion of Russia's power projection far beyond its borders; and the spreading tentacles of international terrorism.

The United States debates its proper role in the world; Europe has come home and apparently intends to stay there. Jean Monnet and the other founding fathers of the European Community made two preeminent bets: that a unified Europe would not again go to war with itself, and that aggregating the power of individual European nations, none of which was strong enough to have a crucial influence on world order, would allow Europe to maintain its historic role in the international system.[143] Unfortunately for the United States, which needs a vital globalist

Europe as a reliable and powerful strategic partner, Monnet and his colleagues lost the second bet.[144]

But instead of trying to coax the Europeans to renew their centuries-old international vocation, the president persistently assaults them, and the long-term effects are deeply worrying. During a meeting of the Group of Seven (G7) in June 2018, Trump, who complained about German trade practices, reportedly threw pieces of candy at German Chancellor Angela Merkel and said, "Don't say I never give you anything," after remarking earlier that month on Twitter that "the people of Germany are turning against their leadership."[145] During the fraught Brexit negotiations, the president claimed that he "actually told [British Prime Minister] Theresa May how to [negotiate a Brexit deal], but she didn't agree, didn't listen to [him]," and he then said that her proposed plan would "kill" a potential U.S.-UK trade deal.[146] In November 2018, when French President Emmanuel Macron suggested that the EU should build an army and improve its military capabilities, Trump mocked the idea, claiming that the French "were starting to learn German in Paris before the U.S. came along."[147] He has threatened via tweet to release captured European Islamic State fighters if the EU did not "take [them] back."[148] At the end of the February 2019 Munich Security Conference, an anonymous German senior official told the *New York Times* that "no one any longer believes that Trump cares about the views or interests of the [European] allies."[149]

Trump appears to resent nearly every aspect of European contributions to the transatlantic relationship, including to NATO, which is the most successful alliance in human history.[150] Now numbering twenty-nine nations, it has been the foundation of transatlantic stability and prosperity for seven decades. It deters an increasingly aggressive Russia and is the crucial central element in ensuring that Europe is at peace with itself and avoiding a war into which the United States would be drawn. The president has most of his "facts" wrong.

Before taking office, he called NATO "obsolete," even though it was playing an important part in easing the transition from the Soviet Union to Russia, aiding U.S. efforts in the war in Afghanistan, and buttressing the democratic practices of its eastern members.[151] He questioned whether the United States would come to the defense of a NATO member were one attacked, even though it has a commitment to do so per Article 5 of the North Atlantic Treaty. He asserted that the population of tiny Montenegro was "very strong" and "very aggressive" and that those dangerous qualities, presumably in combination with a conflict with Russia, could trigger World War III if the

United States kept its treaty obligations.[152] More alarmingly, he has also stressed publicly that he "probably" can pull out of NATO; and, according to some reports, he had privately discussed NATO withdrawal "several times over the course of 2018," claiming that he "did not see the point of the military alliance, which he presented as a drain on the United States."[153]

The president argues that Germany owes "vast sums of money to NATO & the United States must be paid more for the powerful, and very expensive, defense it provides to Germany!" and opines that Germany is a "captive of Russia."[154] But NATO does not work that way. No NATO member owes money to the alliance, for defense or anything else. (The level of German defense spending is shameful, given its extraordinary wealth as well as the renewed dangers posed by Russia. However, calling the Federal Republic of Germany a "captive" of Russia is ludicrous.)

Since Trump's presidential campaign began, he has lumped balance-of-trade issues with U.S. NATO obligations, complaining that "we are spending a fortune on military in order to lose $800 billion [in trade losses]. That doesn't sound like it's smart to me."[155] Trump has continued this rhetoric well into his presidency; at a July 2018 rally, he stated that he would "tell NATO . . . to start paying [its] bills" and lamented that the Europeans "want [the United States] to protect against Russia, and yet they pay billions and billions of dollars to Russia [for gas], and we are the schmucks paying for the whole thing."[156] Just a few days later, leaving for Europe to visit NATO leaders and meet with Vladimir Putin, he stated, "NATO has not treated us fairly. . . . So I have NATO, I have the UK, which is in somewhat turmoil, and I have Putin. Frankly, Putin may be the easiest of them all [to deal with]."[157] In sum, President Trump's threats to abandon U.S. treaty commitments, as well as his affinity for Russia, the primary threat to the security of the European members of the alliance, have shaken the confidence of the other NATO members in the United States' willingness to defend them.

Yet perhaps partly because of his disparaging comments, NATO has begun to reverse its spending decreases and has embarked on reforms, which when completed would improve its ability to defend and reinforce its eastern flank. NATO countries actually began to boost their defense spending in 2014, after Russia illegally annexed Crimea and fomented a civil conflict in eastern Ukraine. But increases among European member states have become more pronounced since Trump took office. In constant 2010 prices, European allies spent $275 billion in 2017 and $288 billion in 2018, compared to $264 billion in 2016 and $254 billion in 2014.[158]

Countries in Eastern Europe had previously planned to reach the goal of spending 2 percent of gross domestic product (GDP) on defense, and several other NATO members that had not done so began to bolster their defense budgets. NATO Secretary-General Jens Stoltenberg specifically noted that Europe "agreed to do more to step up [because of President Trump's demands]—and now we see the results," a projected boost of $100 billion.[159]

In the most recent summit in Brussels in July 2018, all NATO member states concurred with specific measures to improve their ability to respond to crises in Eastern Europe and elsewhere. This has included hiring 1,200 new NATO staff and establishing new joint logistics commands in Ulm, Germany, and Norfolk, Virginia (in addition to facilities already present there), as well as building a dedicated cyberspace operations center in Belgium.[160] Most notably, the alliance has begun efforts to implement the Four Thirties program: "30 [mechanized] battalions, 30 air squadrons and 30 combat vessels, ready to use [after an incident occurs] within 30 days or less."[161] Although this initiative, for which then Secretary of Defense Jim Mattis pushed hard, does not have an implementation timetable, broad support within NATO for the four objectives reflects more robust U.S.-European defense ties.

Moreover, Trump's sympathetic comments about Russia and the uselessness of NATO have not stopped him from proposing large U.S. military spending increases tied to specific initiatives to improve alliance capabilities in Eastern Europe. Building on the Obama-initiated European Deterrence Initiative (EDI) program, which was designed to deter Russian aggression against NATO by improving the alliance's ability to send reinforcements to Eastern Europe, the Defense Department asked for $6.5 billion in funding in fiscal year 2019, compared to just $3.4 billion in fiscal year 2016. The largest increases in the 2019 EDI request were in funds for enhanced readiness (primarily for the buildup of pre-positioned equipment for two armored brigade combat teams and other units in Europe) and in combat infrastructure improvements.[162]

In addition, to shore up its ability to respond to crises in the North Atlantic and to defend its allies, the U.S. Navy formally reinstated the Second Fleet in 2018 and is building its capacity to provide capable forces to Europe.[163] U.S. Special Forces also cooperated with their European NATO counterparts in their largest-ever joint exercise, which featured nearly two thousand personnel.[164] Although Poland's hope to offer $2 billion in exchange for a permanent U.S. military base (which Polish President Andrzej Duda referred to as "Fort Trump") has not moved forward, the United States does rotate combat forces through Poland and operates reconnaissance drones in Eastern Europe from a Polish facility.[165] The State Department under Secretary Pompeo has paid special attention to Eastern Europe, seeking to improve U.S. security, cybersecurity, and energy cooperation with countries there.[166]

From an operational standpoint, NATO today remains more capable of defending its members from Russian aggression than it was in the fifteen years before Trump took office. Both Europe and the United States are doing more to bolster their defense capabilities to deter a wide variety of threats. NATO is stronger in all respects but one: its members' confidence that the others, in particular the United States, will uphold their Article 5 commitments in the event of a war. Although capable senior officials in the Trump administration have done important work for the NATO alliance, President Trump, who sees the treaty as a burden rather than a benefit, has weakened alliance solidarity and could well continue that pattern with his tweets.

This raises the crucial issue of Trump's assault on the psychology of NATO, despite the practical measures the alliance has taken in the past two years to improve its defenses, led by the United States. Ultimately, if NATO fractures because of a lack of confidence in the U.S. security guarantee, these defense enhancements will mean nothing.

*Trump Grade on NATO and European Security Policy: D*

# RUSSIA

Russia's global challenges to American national interests grow.[167] Since Vladimir Putin returned to the presidency in 2012, Moscow has significantly stepped up its efforts to confront the United States and its allies politically and militarily and to counter American influence worldwide. Russia has invaded and annexed Crimea; intervened in and occupied parts of eastern Ukraine; deployed substantial military forces and undertaken a ruthless bombing campaign in Syria to successfully prop up the Bashar al-Assad regime and defeat the American-supported opposition; significantly expanded its armed forces; interfered in the political systems of the United States and European countries; and used the threat of cutting off gas supplies as leverage over the most energy-dependent European states.

Putin has increased military spending; by 2016, Russia spent around $70 billion, or 5.3 percent of GDP, on defense, the highest percentage spent on defense since the Russian Federation emerged in 1991.[168] (The budget has fallen since then, but by less than 10 percent in absolute terms.[169]) In Afghanistan, Moscow has openly admitted to sharing intelligence with the Afghan Taliban since 2015, ostensibly to fight the Islamic State.[170] Russia has also beefed up its military presence in the Arctic, Caucasus, and northern Europe; expanded military exercises, including the September 2017 Zapad exercise of more than seventy thousand troops in western Russia; launched cyberattacks on information systems in the Baltic states and Eastern Europe; built up its nuclear forces; and deployed new midrange missiles, in breach of the 1987 Intermediate-Range Nuclear Forces (INF) Treaty.[171]

A career intelligence officer, Putin is hostile to democratic change anywhere near Russia, paranoid about what he believes are U.S. efforts to oust him, and resentful of American domination of the post–Cold War world. His goals are to weaken the United States, divide it from its European allies, and expand Russian influence in Asia, Europe, the Middle East, and beyond.

This Putin preoccupation stems from the Russian president's strongly held view—shared by a wide range of Russians—that the spread of U.S. regional and global "hegemony" since the end of the Cold War threatens Moscow's vital national interests and deprives Russia of its rightful place on the world stage. In 2007, in a famous speech at the Munich Security Conference, Putin complained that "one state and, of course, first and foremost the United States, has overstepped its national borders in every way" and expressed his hostility to a U.S.-dominated world.[172] Putin finds American foreign policies such as the enlargement of NATO, European missile defense deployments, and support for democracy around the world (and particularly in states near Russia and in Russia itself) to be direct threats.

Because of these Russian policies, the United States and its European treaty allies regrettably are now forced to adopt a policy of neo-containment to protect the sovereignty, security, and democracy of all NATO members; Moscow seeks to undermine all three. Put differently, currently no acceptable grand bargain with Putin is possible that would produce more responsible Russian behavior regarding European and global security and the West. Rather, Putin seems determined to exploit what he regards as the moral and philosophical weakness of the democracies to Russia's strategic advantage. To permit him to do so would produce a geopolitical shift in the global balance of power and put Western values and vital national interests on a downward slope. That should not be allowed to happen.

In the context of all these aggressive Russian actions, Donald Trump's relationship with Vladimir Putin and Russia is a riddle wrapped in a mystery inside an enigma.[173] His most vivid public embrace of Putin, which dramatically reflects his persistent view of the Russian leader and the need "to get along with Russia," was in Helsinki in July 2018.[174] There, he dismissed the unanimous conclusion of the U.S. intelligence community that Russia had intervened in the 2016 U.S. presidential election. Instead, he said he accepted Vladimir Putin's assurance that it was not true. When reporters asked what he thought of the assessments from Director of National Intelligence Daniel Coats and the individual intelligence agencies, he remarked that they "think it's Russia. I have President Putin, he just said it's not Russia. I will say this: I don't see any reason why it would be [Russia]."[175]

Coats immediately rebutted the president's statement: "We have been clear in our assessments of Russian meddling in the 2016 election and their ongoing, pervasive efforts to undermine our democracy, and we will continue to provide unvarnished and objective intelligence in support of our national security."[176] Nicholas Burns, who was U.S. ambassador to NATO and undersecretary of state under George W. Bush, could not "remember a similar episode from modern American presidential history where, when standing beside the person who was our most dangerous adversary, the president continually refused to say a negative word on any subject."[177]

Although Trump has difficulty sorting out the facts of Russian interference in the U.S. electoral processes, the evidence is clear. Since at least 2014, in an effort to influence the election and undermine confidence in American democracy, Russia has hacked private U.S. citizens' and organizations' computers to steal information; released that information in ways designed to affect electoral outcomes and divide Americans; planted and disseminated disinformation in U.S. social media; used its state-funded and state-controlled media networks, such as RT and Sputnik, to spread that disinformation; purchased ads on U.S. social media sites such as Facebook to spread targeted information designed to anger or inspire political and social groups; deployed tens of thousands of bloggers and bots to disseminate disinformation; cooperated with American citizens and possibly the Trump campaign to discredit Trump's opponent in the election, Hillary Rodham Clinton; and probed election-related computer systems in at least twenty-one U.S. states.

Then President-Elect Trump opposed President Obama's December 2016 minimalist retaliatory measures against Russia for these activities, calling on "our country to move on to bigger and better things."[178] Indeed, far from responding to Russia's intervention, Trump has refused even to acknowledge that it occurred, repeatedly calling the

allegations of electoral interference a "hoax" and accusing Clinton sup-
porters of making them up. During the campaign, candidate Trump
repeatedly said he did not think it happened and (somewhat contradic-
torily) suggested that it could have been done by Russia but perhaps
also by China or "somebody sitting on their bed that weighs four hundred pounds."[179]

In July 2017, President Trump even proposed working together
with Russia to create a joint cybersecurity unit; although the unit was
never created, the initiative underscored Trump's vision of Russia as
a potential cyber partner rather than an adversary that had used cyber
tools to attack the United States.[180] And on November 11, 2017, despite
the assessment of his own CIA director that Russia did interfere,
as spelled out in a January 2017 joint intelligence report, President
Trump still claimed that the report was produced by partisan hacks
and asserted that he believed that Putin's repeated denials of interference were sincere.[181]

Throughout his presidency, Trump has in fact demonstrated a curi-
ous affinity for Russia in general and Putin specifically, often praising
the Russian leader and rarely challenging Moscow's policy positions.
Whereas the president's default attitude toward virtually every other
major country in the world is highly critical and he insists that the
United States has been getting a "bad deal," he has consistently shown
sympathy and understanding for Russian perspectives and suggested
it would be "nice if we actually could get along."[182] In November 2017,
Trump said he hoped to find a way to lift sanctions on Russia to promote cooperation, again emphasizing on Twitter that "having a good
relationship with Russia is a good thing, not a bad thing. . . . I want to
solve North Korea, Syria, Ukraine, terrorism, and Russia can greatly
help!"[183] Just before his meeting with Putin in Helsinki, the president
noted that the Russian leader was "very nice to [him]" and that he
was "not [his] enemy. . . . And hopefully, someday, maybe he'll be a
friend."[184] He even excused the Soviet Union's invasion of Afghanistan
in the 1980s, bizarrely stating that it was justified because of a terrorist
threat to Russia.[185]

With the president's persistently sympathetic sentiments regarding
Russia, it is no surprise that his administration has struggled to implement even legally required penalties against Russia for its efforts to interfere with elections in the United States and for its actions in Ukraine,
Syria, and elsewhere.[186] For example, when Congress passed the Countering America's Adversaries Through Sanctions Act (CAATSA),
President Trump called the bill "seriously flawed—particularly because

it encroaches on the executive branch's ability to negotiate."[187] The law required the Trump administration to submit a list of entities involved in the Russian defense and intelligence sectors to be targets of sanctions, and to implement secondary sanctions on firms doing business with these entities by the end of January 2018. Instead, the administration delayed this measure, claiming that imposing sanctions was unnecessary "because the legislation is, in fact, serving as a deterrent."[188]

The Trump team eventually began to enforce the law, and at this writing the State Department lists thirty-six defense-related and forty-eight intelligence-related entities as groups that others could face secondary sanctions for conducting "significant transaction[s]" with.[189] It designated and sanctioned twenty-four targets in March 2018, twenty-four individuals and the companies they controlled in April 2018, eight targets in June 2018, thirty-three targets in September 2018, and sixteen individuals in December 2018 under CAATSA for cybersecurity violations.[190] However, in December 2018, the Trump administration sought permission to lift CAATSA sanctions that had been placed on three companies (En+, EuroSibEnergo JSC, and Rusal) owned by Russian oligarch Oleg Deripaska for his involvement in Russian global "malign activity." Although the Treasury Department announced that the sanctions would be lifted when Deripaska reduced his "ownership and control" of his firms, he still maintains a majority stake in at least one of the sanctioned firms.[191] On January 27, 2019, despite an effort from Senate Democrats to stop the move, the United States lifted CAATSA sanctions on the three companies, allowing the rest of the world to do business with them.[192]

To its credit, the Trump administration has taken some actions that were not required by law. For example, the Justice Department forced state-owned news outlet RT America to register as a foreign agent in November 2017, and in the following month the administration added fifty-two individuals, many of them Russian, to the list of sanctioned human rights abusers under the Magnitsky Act.[193] The Trump team has also frequently pursued charges in absentia against Russians for a wide variety of destabilizing activities. The Justice Department indicted three Russians in March 2017 for the hack of Yahoo; sixteen Russian individuals and companies in February 2018 for 2016 election interference; twelve Russian intelligence agents in July 2018 for hacking the Clinton campaign; and seven agents of the Russian military intelligence service, known as GRU, in October 2018 for other malicious cyber activity.[194] In response to the poisoning of Russian ex–double agent Sergei Skripal and his daughter in Salisbury, England, the administration imposed sanctions on the individuals involved, banned all remaining exports of potential dual-use items to Russia, expelled sixty Russian diplomats from the United States, and closed the Russian consulate in Seattle.[195] Nevertheless, despite the president's assertions that he has been "tougher on Russia than any president, maybe ever," these measures are far too small to be proportional to Moscow's many destabilizing actions, and are as weak in this regard as were those of President Obama.[196]

An exception to this inadequate approach to Russia has been President Trump's justifiable decision to withdraw from the INF Treaty. After imposing import restrictions on two Russian defense companies for violations of the agreement a year earlier, in December 2018 Secretary Pompeo gave Russia a sixty-day notice that the United States would cease to abide by the treaty's obligations unless Russia came back into compliance.[197] Russia has violated the treaty with the Novator 9M729 intermediate-range missile; and China, the United States' most powerful strategic threat, is not bound by the agreement's limitations.[198]

Moscow has denied that its weapons systems violate treaty specifications and did not change its deployments before the February deadline. Secretary Pompeo stated that effective February 2, the United States suspended participation in the agreement and would permanently leave the agreement if Russia did not go back into compliance within six months. Putin announced that Russia would not seek to abide by the treaty's rules.[199] It is regrettable that the INF Treaty will end its role as a stabilizing factor in European security, but the United States cannot accept persistent Russian violations of any arms control agreement.[200] If it did, negotiated arms limitation would end as an instrument of great power conciliation, a reality recognized as far back as the Nixon administration.

Another important area in which the Trump administration has pushed back against Russian actions is Ukraine.[201] It has gone further than the Obama administration in supporting that nation's struggle against Russian-backed separatist forces, particularly in terms of military assistance. In December 2017, the administration announced that it would send lethal defensive aid to Ukraine and delivered sniper rifles and other small arms. It followed up in April 2018 by delivering 37 Javelin anti-tank rocket launchers and 210 rockets. Congress has authorized $250 million to be spent on additional lethal aid sales in 2019, and U.S. Special Representative for Ukraine Kurt Volker stated that the United States was "look[ing] at air defense" and other support for the Ukrainian Air Force and Navy.[202] In July 2018, the Defense Department also released $200 million in nonlethal defense aid to

Ukraine, including secure communications, night vision, and combat medical equipment.[203]

Moreover, in the 2018 State and Foreign Operations Appropriations Bill, Congress, with the administration's support, authorized $420.7 million in economic assistance to Ukraine, $10 million more than the previous year.[204] Finally, U.S. troops have participated in multiple military training activities with the Ukrainians since Trump took office, such as the September 2017 Rapid Trident air exercise and the October 2018 Clear Sky exercise.[205] Nevertheless, Putin has continued his efforts to weaken and dismember Ukraine. In November 2018, Russian ships captured three Ukrainian vessels in the Black Sea as part of an effort to economically isolate the country's east, and the United States took no punitive action against Moscow beyond increasing naval aid to Ukraine by only $10 million and canceling a planned Trump-Putin meeting at a Group of Twenty summit in Argentina.[206]

Overall, the Trump administration's response to the Russian challenge has been deficient. The president's policy objective seems, with the exception of INF withdrawal and Ukraine, to be to put as little pressure on Moscow as possible regarding its destabilizing foreign policies. Unfortunately for U.S. national interests, he has had some success in this regard.

It is striking, when examining the list of U.S. retaliatory measures, how little Russia has been punished during Trump's presidency for its massive interference in the U.S. electoral process, its many destabilizing activities in Eurasia and beyond, and Putin's determination to undermine America's standing and influence around the globe. The United States is militarily and economically superior to Russia, and yet it has struggled to respond to Russia's actions.[207] Because of this, tough diplomatic interaction between senior U.S. officials and Moscow is unlikely to have much effect on Putin, since he knows he has a friend who goes to work every morning in the Oval Office. It does not take a weatherman to know which way the wind is blowing from the White House regarding Russia. One wonders why.

*Trump Grade on Russia Policy: F*

# IRAN

It is difficult to find something uplifting to write about the Middle East today. Violence in Syria and Yemen is ongoing. Saudi Arabia's relations with the United States and the West are in difficulty. Iraq is structurally unstable. The two-state solution is in prolonged suspended animation. Russia is back in the Middle East in a destructive way for the first time in more than four decades. Iran's hegemonic ambitions are not slowing. Nuclear proliferation (or a war to stop it) could be only a few years away. The Trump administration, in the context of meeting the challenges of the rise of Chinese power in Asia, seems determined to reduce its commitments to the region to some degree, but it remains uncertain where, when, and how. In this evolving Middle East maelstrom the president needs to find a strategic compass to chart the way in the decade ahead, but such an enduring approach to any issue is not Trump's strength, so he will be graded on where administration policies stand at this writing.

The Obama administration badly negotiated the Joint Comprehensive Plan of Action (JCPOA) to constrain Iran's nuclear activities: it made clear to the Iranians that the United States wanted the accord more than they did and that it would not accept a breakdown of the talks.[208] Senator Tom Cotton (R-AR) has correctly identified three major terminal flaws in the agreement:

> Sunsets: At year eight of the deal, restrictions on Iran's nuclear program begin to "sunset," allowing Iran to steadily industrialize its uranium enrichment program. By year fifteen, all restrictions expire, bringing Iran to the brink of nuclear breakout.

Verification: The JCPOA fails to provide the International Atomic Energy Agency (IAEA) necessary authority to verify Iran's compliance with the agreement.

Research and Development: The JCPOA allows Iran to develop advanced centrifuges, which dramatically reduces the time needed to produce a nuclear weapon.[209]

The accord also does not stop Iran from testing ballistic missiles and supporting terrorists and insurgents in Lebanon, Yemen, and across the Middle East; those constraints were several bridges too far to achieve in this negotiation. Finally, the lifting of sanctions gave Iran more resources to pursue its goal of regional hegemony. Given the substantial leverage that the United States had over Iran in this negotiation, Jim Baker, Henry Kissinger, or George Shultz could have produced a better deal to permanently constrain Iran's nuclear weapons potential.

Because of these perceived terminal weaknesses and others, the Trump administration withdrew from the JCPOA in May 2018. The president said the United States was pulling out of the accord to send a message that it "no longer makes empty threats."[210] Although the president has asserted that Iran poses a greater immediate danger than U.S. intelligence agencies suggest, the U.S. withdrawal from the nuclear deal has not yet exacerbated that threat.[211] So far, sanctions have not led to a spike in oil prices as many predicted, Iran has complied with the terms of the JCPOA, and European businesses are leaving Iran even as allied governments seek to save the accord. In short, none of the dangerous consequences that critics envisioned post-JCPOA have materialized.

But the administration's demands to Tehran are effectively impossible for Iran to accommodate without fundamentally changing its leadership and system of government.[212] The president is requiring regime change in Iran without calling it that, and, unsurprisingly, the mullahs do not agree. Historically, pressure has been the only way to coerce Iran to constrain its behavior (including its nuclear weapons program), so it is unclear what the president will do if, instead of succumbing, Iran resumes work on its nuclear programs.

The United States has sped up programs involving cyberattacks and sneaking defective components into Iran to derail its missile program, but such efforts are unlikely to forestall Iran's nuclear and missile development forever. The president should now begin U.S.-European discussions on what conditions—especially limits on the sunset clauses—need to be met for the United States to reenter the JCPOA.[213] The administration also has not effectively coordinated, with allies and European partners, responses to Iran's attempts to gain hegemony across the Middle East.[214]

If Tehran returns to enhancing its nuclear capabilities, an attack on Iran's nuclear facilities could be the only course left for President Trump. Success would depend on as-yet-unseen intense and skillful coordination within his administration. Such an attack would be opposed by nearly the entire world, except Israel and Saudi Arabia; filled with uncertainties, including about the effectiveness of the attack; and rife with unintended consequences that the president is in no position to assess. Nearly everything could go wrong with such an attack.

In sum, Trump withdrew from a flawed agreement but has no considered strategy to accomplish his ambitious goals and avoid conflict regarding Iran's nuclear potential. Trump has likely not thought through the policies and strategies he would adopt if he were to initiate a long war with Iran. It is also highly unclear what U.S. policy will be toward Tehran on the nuclear issue during the rest of the president's time in office.

*Trump Grade on Iran Policy: C*

# SYRIA

The president announced in a video posted on Twitter on December 19, 2018, that the United States "won against ISIS" and that "our boys, our young women, our men — they're all coming back, and they're coming back now."[215] He had said earlier, "I want to get out. I want to bring our troops back home. I want to start rebuilding our nation."[216]

Most of the government's national security establishment, led by then Secretary of Defense Jim Mattis, as well as the media, fell on the president like a ton of bricks after these public statements regarding U.S. troop withdrawal from Syria, again displaying the incoherence of the administration's policy process.[217] They said Trump's announcement was irresponsible, would allow the Russians and Iranians a free hand in Syria, and repeated President Obama's mistake of withdrawing U.S. troops from Iraq before the enemy was wholly defeated. At this writing, Trump may have reluctantly stepped back from following through on his instinct to withdraw all U.S. troops from Syria and may leave four hundred behind.[218] But he should not step back. He is right and his critics are wrong.[219]

The original mission of U.S. forces deployed in Syria was to defeat the territorial version of the Islamic State. This has largely been accomplished, thus fully justifying a U.S. troop withdrawal.[220] If a serious Islamic State threat reignited in Syria, U.S. troops based in Iraq could attack Islamic State combatants in Syria as the need arose.[221] However, if mission creep changes U.S. combat objectives to require that Islamic State fighters or sympathizers cannot find refuge anywhere in Syria, then American troop deployment in Syria, whose government opposes a U.S. military presence, would never end, especially given Assad's brutal policies toward Syria's citizens.[222] In such a situation, U.S. security personnel would be killed for territory that has no importance to the United States.[223] Moreover, surely the failed experiments in Afghanistan and Iraq have expended Washington's appetite for nation-building in faraway places. Finally, protecting the Syrian Kurds from Assad and Turkey's Erdogan in perpetuity cannot be a preeminent U.S. national security objective. The Kurds will eventually have to make the best deal they can with Assad and Erdogan, and U.S. military deployments in Syria only postpone that day.

Some security experts assert that a U.S. troop withdrawal would lead to an Iranian and Russian victory in Syria.[224] Here is a news flash from the battle space: Iran and Russia have already prevailed in Syria. Assisted by Russian air power and foreign Shiite troops, Assad has won the civil war and will remain in power for the foreseeable future. The Obama administration fecklessly attempted regime change in Syria and was shown to have been holding a busted flush.[225] The notion that a few thousand U.S. troops in northeastern Syria will balance Iran's comprehensive penetration of the Syrian government and society is a fantasy.[226] Iran and Russia are in Syria to stay, and the United States can do nothing about it. But that unfortunate development does not have to threaten important American equities in the Middle East, if Washington takes the necessary steps to shore up its relationships with regional partners, beginning with Saudi Arabia. Withdrawing U.S. troops from Syria (and Afghanistan) carries some risk because a major terrorist attack against the United States could originate there, instead of Germany (as in 9/11), Pakistan, Somalia, or the United States itself. But virtually any foreign policy decision carries some risk, and systematically avoiding such incalculables is a recipe for sclerotic policies that cling to the status quo far past their effectiveness.

*Trump Grade on Syria Policy: B+*

# SAUDI ARABIA

Saudi Arabia is America's longest-standing ally in the Middle East, even though the kingdom is not a partner made in heaven for the United States. Its citizens, including Osama bin Laden, have been involved in numerous terrorist attacks against the United States, most consequentially on 9/11. Saudi Arabia is not a democracy. It fuels Islamist extremism far beyond its borders through its exports of ultraconservative Wahhabi religious doctrine. Its human rights practices are often deplorable, and occasionally medieval. Its treatment of women is unacceptable. It has used oil in the past as a weapon against U.S. national interests. It bombs innocent civilians in Yemen. It occasionally threatens to acquire nuclear weapons. It promises huge sums of money to worthy regional actors, and then often fails to deliver. It blockades Qatar. And now, Crown Prince Mohammed bin Salman apparently ordered the execution in Istanbul of journalist and *Washington Post* columnist Jamal Khashoggi.[227]

All this has produced a flood of U.S. criticism of Saudi Arabia and calls to sanction Riyadh, end U.S.-Saudi military cooperation in Yemen, cut off arms sales, and overall rupture the intensity and substance of the bilateral relationship. As the *Washington Post* editorial page put it, "Who Needs Saudi Arabia?"[228]

The president's answer is that the United States does, and he is right.[229] The murder of Khashoggi, including its barbarous method, was as abhorrent as it was stupid. But bin Salman is the most powerful man in Saudi Arabia and its likely future king. At this writing, he is thirty-three years old and could easily rule the kingdom for the next four decades and beyond, well after Trump and many of his current critics are dead. Thus the United States will most likely have to deal with him for a long time. Making an enemy of him now is not a good idea, especially given the many other challenges the United States faces in the region.

Moreover, Mohammed bin Salman, though authoritarian, espouses a moderate and modern message (in Saudi terms) and is the leader most likely to keep extremist forces from gaining power and influence in the kingdom. An unstable Saudi Arabia would be a preeminent source of potential terrorists and radical ideology. Further, without Saudi Arabia, the United States cannot have a coherent and effective policy to counter Iran's hegemonic activities in the Middle East. No other Arab state could be the hub of such an indispensable U.S. effort. And although the United States has dramatically reduced its dependence on Saudi oil, the global economy and the economies of U.S. treaty allies depend on energy from the kingdom.[230]

In addition, the U.S. security relationship with Saudi Arabia goes well beyond arms sales: it also involves intense intelligence community collaboration and significant financing for counterterrorist campaigns.[231] To add to the list, Mohammed bin Salman has a different and more benign view toward Israel than do many other Arab rulers, and as former Israeli Prime Minister Ehud Olmert observes, "Saudi Arabia is the country that in the end will determine the ability of the Arabs to reach a compromise with Israel."[232] Moreover, without reliable U.S. military protection, Riyadh might well seek to acquire nuclear weapons. Finally, if the United States weakens its partnership with Saudi Arabia, U.S. adversaries China and Russia will fill the vacuum, including by providing the kingdom with nuclear reactors without full-scope safeguards—a line Riyadh should not cross.

Saudi Arabia needs the United States at least as much as the United States needs it. Washington should be stout in defending its equities in dealing with Riyadh. But this mutual dependence is an enduring strength of the bilateral relationship. It should not be damaged because of Saudi Arabia's sometimes problematic policies.

*Trump Grade on Saudi Arabia Policy: B+*

# ISRAEL

U.S. defense, intelligence, and diplomatic cooperation with Israel is wider and deeper than ever before. During the Trump presidency, Congress codified into law an Obama-era memorandum of understanding for defense aid to Israel; the United States is now committed to providing Israel $38 billion over ten years. This is the largest-ever defense-related transfer to Israel.[233] The president has supplemented this aid with $705 million in support for Israeli missile defense systems.[234] Trump's decision to move the U.S. embassy to Jerusalem was the right step to take and did not produce the harms that critics predicted, although it would have been wise for the administration to try to trade moving the embassy for no further Israeli settlement activity beyond the current settlement blocs on the West Bank. In another show of support, Trump announced via Twitter on March 21, 2019, that "after 52 years it is time for the United States to fully recognize Israel's Sovereignty over the Golan Heights, which is of critical strategic and security importance to the State of Israel and Regional Stability," a measure that if carried out will further roil the Middle East. The administration has been a fierce defender of Israel within the UN system, which maintains a structural bias against Israel. Trump also stopped ineffective Obama-era efforts to put serious pressure on Israel for its failure to improve the lives of Palestinians, which occurred during a stalemate in the progress toward a two-state solution because of domestic political realities on both sides.

The only weakness in Trump's approach to Israel again originates in his odd relationship with Putin and Russia. Trump leaves Jerusalem alone to negotiate with Moscow over the future of Iran's increasingly threatening military presence in Syria. This matters because if Tehran seeks to further arm and train Israel's enemies in Syria, Jerusalem will not allow a replication of Iran's massive weaponizing of Hezbollah in

Lebanon. This could lead to conflict between Israel and Iran, first in Syria; then, if Iran attacks Israel, Israel might strike Iran and initiate a wider war, into which the United States would inevitably be drawn. Here, as in so many areas, diplomacy is not a tool of President Trump's foreign policy.

Nevertheless, Trump is as supportive of Israel as any American president since 1948, and more so than most of his predecessors. What matters most in the U.S. approach to Israel is, and always has been, the United States' military contribution to Israel's safety and security. And in that domain, the president is unsurpassed.

*Trump Grade on Israel Policy: B*

# AFGHANISTAN

Young Americans who were not born when the United States first sent troops to Afghanistan after 9/11 are now enlisting in the military and face possible deployment there. The president is right to want to end the U.S. combat role in the "forever war" and to withdraw all U.S. troops from Afghanistan.[235] As he has put it, "I inherited a total mess in Syria and Afghanistan, the 'Endless Wars' of unlimited spending and death. During my campaign I said, very strongly, that these wars must finally end."[236] However, his determination to do so unfortunately appears to be weakening under the constant criticism he is receiving from his own administration, Congress, and outside experts.[237]

In his 2019 State of the Union speech, he tied such a departure of U.S. troops to progress in the peace negotiations, a recipe for indefinite U.S. deployments in Afghanistan.[238] The United States has spent over $1 trillion on the war, and over two thousand U.S. soldiers have been killed and twenty thousand wounded.[239] Notwithstanding that enormous eighteen-year U.S. investment, Council on Foreign Relations President Richard Haass sees a "slowly deteriorating stalemate," with "no military victory" possible.[240] He believes negotiations are unlikely to succeed, simply because the Taliban is convinced it can outlast the United States and NATO. (As the Taliban says, "NATO has the watches but we have the time."[241])

Many of President Trump's critics agree that U.S. involvement in the war in Afghanistan should come to an end, but later, not now.[242] The problem is that the "do it later" horizon keeps receding, so that the net effect is an indefinite U.S. combat commitment to Afghanistan.[243] As Henry Kissinger has observed, "To other nations, Utopia is a blessed past never to be recovered. For Americans, it is just beyond the horizon."[244] (One might add, just beyond the Afghan horizon.)

Trump's detractors apparently believe that the United States should stay the course in Afghanistan for as long as it takes to end the Taliban military threat and leave behind a stable coalition government.[245] They think Washington should continue this commitment, despite the lack of U.S. vital national interests related to Afghanistan.[246] But as C. J. Chivers of the *New York Times* persuasively argues, these policies "have not succeeded," and the wars have proven "astonishingly expensive" and "strategically incoherent."[247]

According to a July 2018 assessment from the Department of Defense:

> The al-Qa'ida threat to the United States and its allies and partners has decreased, and the few remaining al-Qa'ida core members are focused on their own survival.... Some lower- and mid-level Taliban leaders provide limited support to al-Qa'ida; however, there is no evidence of strategic ties between the two organizations and the Taliban likely seeks to maintain distance from al-Qa'ida.[248]

The original U.S. military objective in Afghanistan was to eliminate al-Qaeda, not the Afghan Taliban. The United States has largely accomplished its original goal.

However, those who oppose U.S. troop withdrawal from Afghanistan argue that withdrawal would reinvigorate al-Qaeda and the Islamic State, and that the United States, with insufficient intelligence generated from the battle space, would face a renewed major terrorist threat to the homeland. But there would be limited or no practical difference if the current al-Qaeda concentrations in Pakistan moved the one hundred miles or so from the tribal areas across the border into Afghanistan.[249] It is not worth the United States participating in an indefinite ground war and spending billions more dollars to try to prevent that from happening. The United States can now attack al-Qaeda targets on both sides of the border, which was not the case in the years before 9/11, when the United States was passive as al-Qaeda built up its terrorist infrastructure. And a repeat of a 2001-type terrorist attack on the homeland could be planned anywhere.

Although applied history is a perilous venture, as Richard Neustadt and Ernest May documented in their classic, *Thinking in Time*, there are disconcerting similarities between the Vietnam and Afghanistan wars.[250] The Taliban does not have a superpower sponsor, but the United States is again fighting on the ground in Asia; is largely ignorant of the history of the country; is supporting a corrupt government;

is negotiating with the adversary without the host government, thus generating substantial suspicion of a U.S. sellout, with President Ashraf Ghani of Afghanistan playing the role of President Nguyen Van Thieu of South Vietnam; is underestimating the enemy's determination to reach its fundamental objectives; is failing to sufficiently understand and cultivate the people it is seeking to protect; is unsuccessfully attempting to train an army that could stand up to the adversary; and is facing an implacable foe with a sanctuary just outside the country.[251]

A RAND Corporation study on Afghanistan recently argued that winning may not be an available option, but losing certainly is. A precipitous departure, no matter how rationalized, will mean choosing to lose. The result, the study contends, would be a blow to American credibility, the weakening of deterrence and the value of U.S. reassurance elsewhere, an increased terrorist threat emanating from the Afghan region, and the distinct possibility of a necessary return there under worse conditions.[252]

In 1965, Secretary of State Dean Rusk wrote to President Johnson:

> There can be no serious debate about the fact that we have a commitment to assist the South Vietnamese to resist aggression from the North. . . . The integrity of the U.S. commitment is the principal pillar of peace throughout the world. . . . So long as the South Vietnamese are prepared to fight for themselves, we cannot abandon them without disaster to peace and to our interests throughout the world.[253]

It was not true in Vietnam then, and, despite RAND's assertions, it is not true in Afghanistan now.

There is current talk that the Taliban might agree with the U.S. and Afghan governments to a cease-fire with forces in place on the way to a final peace agreement and a coalition government in Kabul, along with the withdrawal of U.S. forces.[254] That seems an unlikely recipe for peace and stability in Afghanistan.[255] Trump's own tendencies make this process even more tenuous; as former Afghanistan negotiator James Dobbins has observed, "I don't think he [Zalmay Khalilzad, who is leading the current negotiations with the Taliban] knows what Trump's going to do. . . . He was in negotiations when Trump made his announcement about [halving] the troops. He was as blindsided as anybody."[256]

The president is not the only issue, however. Again, the Vietnam analogy comes to mind. Henry Kissinger reached an agreement with

Le Duc Tho in January 1973 on similar terms—cease-fire in place, coalition government, and the withdrawal of U.S. forces. Two years later, the enemy entered Saigon and Americans fled to safety from the roof of the U.S. embassy. The Taliban is no more likely than North Vietnam to abide by the terms of such an accord. Some of the U.S. proponents of a peace deal could be simply seeking a decent interval for the United States until Kabul falls to the Taliban.[257]

As Leon Panetta said a decade ago about Taliban behavior when he headed the CIA,

> We have seen no evidence that they are truly interested in reconciliation where they would surrender their arms, where they would denounce al-Qaeda, where they would really try to become part of that society. We have seen no evidence of that and very frankly my view is that with regards to reconciliation unless they're convinced the United States is going to win and that they are going to be defeated, I think it is very difficult to proceed with a reconciliation that is going to be meaningful.[258]

In other words, there is no need to negotiate seriously when you are winning.

On December 20, 2018, the president ordered the reduction of American forces in Afghanistan, with more than seven thousand of the fourteen thousand troops on the ground expected to return to the United States.[259] Implementation appears to have been delayed. In early February 2019, Acting Secretary of Defense Patrick Shanahan said he had not received orders to withdraw forces from Afghanistan.[260] On February 14, 2019, following Shanahan's first meeting with NATO defense ministers, he promised cooperation with allies and stated that "there will be no unilateral troop reductions."[261] At this writing, this troop reduction appears to be on hold while U.S. diplomats conduct peace talks with the Taliban.[262]

In all of this, one is reminded of the White Queen's comment: "Why, sometimes I've believed as many as six impossible things before breakfast."[263] Current U.S. policy in the Afghanistan conflict does not make strategic sense.[264] Historians will not understand why the United States fought a war in Afghanistan for nearly eighteen years after 9/11. Current U.S. policymakers will not remember twenty years from now why it was so important to defend Kandahar and why they spoke as if the fate of the civilized world depended on U.S. success in Afghanistan, whose territory has no strategic importance. In two decades, these individuals serving at the top of the Bush, Obama, and Trump administrations will likely not still find the grand importance of Afghanistan self-evident. Instead, they might ask, as other American policymakers on other issues have questioned before them, "How in God's name did we continue to do that?"[265]

*Trump Grade on Afghanistan Policy: B+*

# INDIA

New Delhi saw foreign policy opportunities in Trump's victory.[266] Here was an American president who might be susceptible to Prime Minister Narendra Modi's charms and consequently forge a close relationship with him; be more restrained in using force abroad while continuing to protect the rules-based international system, thus giving India more sway to advance its own vision of a multipolar global order; seek to improve relations with Moscow, a longtime Indian ally, thereby aiding India's resolve to avoid choosing between the United States and Russia; put less pressure on India regarding climate change and peace with Pakistan; and—most important—take robust measures to check the threatening dimensions of China's increasing power.

This last issue most preoccupies Indian strategists both inside and outside the government. New Delhi is convinced that China is pursuing policies to replace the United States as the primary power in Asia, and that such a development would be exceedingly bad for India.[267] As one senior Indian policymaker privately stressed, "The most fundamental issue of world order is the rise of China, and it is so momentous that it should make every other government reexamine the basic principles of its foreign policy."[268]

President Trump's inclinations, as conveyed through his South Asia strategy, which accords primacy to India; his release of advanced weapons systems, such as unmanned aerial vehicles, for sale to New Delhi; and his decision to treat India on par with NATO allies where strategic technology release is concerned are all viewed as favorable toward India.[269] New Delhi has, accordingly, responded with bold initiatives of its own. Although it has not entirely endorsed the Trump administration's Indo-Pacific strategy, it has applauded the strategy's declared vision of a "free and open" Indo-Pacific region—a concept first articulated by Japan's Prime Minister Shinzo Abe, with whom Prime Minister Modi enjoys an exceptionally close relationship.[270]

In addition, India has quietly—and sometimes not so quietly—begun to cooperate militarily with the United States in significant ways even in peacetime. Today, driven again by common concerns about China, Washington and New Delhi have begun to exchange serious intelligence information, undertake ambitious combined military exercises, and discuss the acquisition of advanced military technologies that would help both states cope with the expanding Chinese military presence, especially in the Indian Ocean. In September 2018, after a meeting between the U.S. secretaries of defense and state and the Indian ministers of defense and external affairs, the two countries signed the Communications Compatibility and Security Agreement, a deal that allows the United States to share advanced secure communications technology and that the Obama administration could not finalize.[271]

Although these initiatives still have far to go, it is significant that they have begun—especially for a country that not too long ago swore eternal fealty to nonalignment. These evolutionary but significant shifts in India's strategic posture have been driven by its own national interests, but in every instance they advance America's strategic objectives as well.[272] This transformation in Indian policy is grounded in the conviction that though improved relations with China are desirable, there is no assurance that they will suffice to protect Indian security in the face of growing Chinese power. Only strong security ties with the United States—in tandem with other important countries such as France, Israel, Japan, and Russia—can provide such comfort at a time when India is still some distance away from realizing its own great power ambitions.

In short, the Trump administration has maintained the success story of U.S.-India relations initiated by George W. Bush. Differences remain in the bilateral relationship over Russia, Iran, and visas; and on March 4, 2019, Trump notified Congress that the United States intends to stop preferential treatment for Indian goods that now enter the country duty-free. [273] But the president deserves credit for promoting strategic ties with India in a sustained manner.

*Trump Grade on India Policy: B+*

# VENEZUELA

Venezuela faces a terrible humanitarian disaster that is spilling over to its neighbors and destabilizing the region. Its people and economy are in a death spiral that began when Caracas's corrupt strongman, Nicolas Maduro, succeeded populist socialist leader Hugo Chavez. Venezuela was once the richest economy in Latin America and a prosperous, wealthy, democratic country, but International Monetary Fund projections of hyperinflation topped 1.3 million percent last year, with 10 million percent projected this year.[274]

Despite having the world's largest proven oil reserves, Venezuela has negative growth.[275] People are starving—Venezuelans have been surviving on garbage bins and eating dogs, cats, and pigeons for the last two years.[276] Venezuela's humanitarian crisis is dire: Three million refugees and migrants have left.[277] Three thousand people cross the borders into neighboring Colombia every day—the worst migration crisis in the region's history.[278]

More than fifty countries, including the United States, Canada, and nearly all of Latin America and Europe, have condemned the Maduro regime and recognized Juan Guaido, leader of the opposition and the National Assembly, as interim president, in line with Venezuela's constitution.[279]

The Trump administration's current policy toward the crisis in Venezuela at this writing seems as if it is being formulated and implemented by a different administration. The policy has not been undermined by presidential tweets. The president has not mixed his goals in the crisis with his trade objectives. The policy has been well conceived and explained. The United States is working with Latin American partners, such as the Organization of American States and the Lima Group, to provide emergency humanitarian assistance.[280] This policy coherence is inconsistent with administration actions toward most other issues.

At the same time, Trump has indicated, unwisely, that using military force remains a live option.[281] The last thing the United States needs is to become embroiled in another military action unrelated to American vital national interests.

*Trump Grade on Venezuela Policy: B+*

# TRADE

From the moment he took office, and even during the 2016 campaign, Donald Trump has confronted America's allies, friends, and China with every manner of complaint and insult regarding their trade relations with the United States.[282] In his inaugural address, President Trump promised to "protect our borders from the ravages of other countries making our products, stealing our companies, and destroying our jobs," adding that "protection will lead to great prosperity and strength."[283]

He often attacks U.S. ally Germany, reportedly stating at one point that the Germans were "very bad" because of "the millions of cars they're selling in the U.S."[284] When Canadian Prime Minister Justin Trudeau called out Trump's trade policies, the president publicly described him as "very dishonest & weak" and refused to sign a joint G7 communiqué endorsing shared liberal values because of his notion "that Canada is charging massive Tariffs to our U.S. farmers, workers and companies."[285] On China, he famously stated that the United States could not "continue to allow China to rape our country" with its trade practices.[286] Protests from even his closest advisors could not shake his view that for decades other nations have taken advantage of Washington through its innocence, stupidity, and incompetence.[287]

Trump seems to believe that a trade deficit means that other countries are taking more from the United States than the United States is getting from them. He dismisses the concept that trade deficits are related to internal U.S. dynamics (i.e., that they occur when the United States spends more than it saves) and that the response is therefore not to renegotiate individual trade deals. And he seems not to anticipate that solving a bilateral deficit in one area will make other bilateral deficits worse.

In his first year, Trump heard opposing voices within his administration, but they have since departed and he has now mostly surrounded himself with advisors who share his distorted views on the subject.[288] They assert that trade deficits damage the U.S. economy and that eliminating them by negotiating better terms on trade agreements will increase domestic growth. Such a concept defies basic economic theory, but this has not reduced the passion and intensity of their convictions.[289]

Contrary to the assertions of Peter Navarro, assistant to the president and director of the Office of Trade and Manufacturing Policy, imports do not decrease GDP. Imports are subtracted in calculating GDP to avoid counting foreign production, because imports increase consumption and investment.[290] Economists note that U.S. trade deficits arise when America spends more than it saves and receives foreign investment to make up the difference; other factors like the dollar's strength also contribute.[291] In practice, such deficits tend to be higher when the economy is strong, as consumers have more to spend on imports and there are more foreign investment opportunities.[292] Protectionist measures to correct bilateral imbalances harm the United States economically without reducing the aggregate deficit.[293]

With these faulty concepts driving his thinking, in March 2018 President Trump used Section 232 of the Trade Expansion Act to justify a 25 percent tariff on steel and a 10 percent tariff on aluminum.[294] He claimed that these were necessary because of a "national security threat," in that foreign competition could shrink the U.S. steel industry to the point where the U.S. military would be unable to meet defense requirements, an assertion that the Pentagon disputed. A Department of Defense memorandum to the Commerce Department noted that "U.S. military requirements for steel and aluminum each only represent about 3 percent of U.S. production. Therefore, DoD does not believe that the findings in the reports impact the ability of DoD programs to acquire the steel or aluminum necessary to meet national defense requirements."[295] Although he permanently exempted Argentina, Australia, and Brazil from steel duties, on May 31, 2018, Trump announced tariffs on Canada, Mexico, and the European Union. These tariffs remain in place at this writing.[296]

In addition, the president reportedly threatened to unilaterally withdraw from the U.S.-Korea Free Trade Agreement (KORUS)—but, according to Bob Woodward, he ended up not doing so because economic advisor Gary Cohn took the order off his desk so Trump would forget to sign it.[297] To meet the president's concerns, U.S. Trade Representative Robert Lighthizer ultimately negotiated a few minor changes to the agreement: the United States can import more vehicles to South Korea that do not meet Korean industry standards, and South Korea agreed to reduce its steel exports to the United States.[298] This mostly cosmetic change satisfied Trump, and South Korea was exempted from the global tariffs.

During the 2016 presidential campaign, candidate Trump repeatedly called NAFTA "the worst trade deal . . . ever signed anywhere" and blamed it for the loss of thousands of American jobs.[299] He also stated that the TPP, the planned twelve-nation trade agreement that would have decreased tariffs in many Asian countries, would be even worse.[300] The Monday after his inauguration, President Trump withdrew the United States from the TPP.

President Trump intended to announce U.S. withdrawal from NAFTA on April 29, 2017, the hundredth day of his presidency. However, most of the members of his cabinet (including otherwise pro-tariff Wilbur Ross) urged him not to do so, and after talking with Prime Minister Justin Trudeau of Canada and then President Enrique Pena Nieto of Mexico, Trump reconsidered and agreed to begin a renegotiation of the accord instead.[301] Trump periodically threatened to withdraw from NAFTA throughout 2017 and 2018 but never acted on it.

Lighthizer began the NAFTA renegotiation process and aimed to briskly conclude a deal. But sticking points, including Washington's insistence that a large percentage of component parts of cars should come from the United States rather than from any of the countries in the free-trade area, delayed the process.[302]

President Trump removed the Canadian and Mexican exemptions to the March global steel and aluminum tariffs on May 31, 2018; they promptly placed retaliatory tariffs on U.S. goods.[303] After more than nine rounds of talks, the sides finally concluded the U.S.-Mexico-Canada Agreement (USMCA) to replace NAFTA on November 30, 2018.[304]

The accord has not yet been ratified by a skeptical Senate, and tariffs remain in place. USMCA is similar to NAFTA but includes some important exceptions for the auto industry: one, 75 percent of cars' content would have to be from any of the three members to avoid tariffs, up from 62.5 percent; and two, 40 to 45 percent of the regional content would have to be made by workers earning sixteen dollars per hour (a step that would be phased in over five years).[305]

From the U.S. point of view, this agreement is certainly better than no deal. But the arrangement is unlikely to create more jobs in the United States than maintaining NAFTA would have done, and President Trump got far less in this negotiation than his inflated rhetoric demanded. To cite just one example, instead of hiring more American or Canadian workers to meet the wage requirements or forcing Mexico to pay its workers more, auto producers will likely not want to make costly changes to their complex supply chains and will instead pay the tariffs that foreign car exporters are charged to enter the North American market.[306] This will slightly increase car prices but do little to affect hiring patterns.

In addition to these other trade trials and tribulations, the president apparently likes nothing about the European Union. As he has succinctly stated, "I think the European Union is a foe, [given] what they do to us in trade."[307] He believes that the EU by design makes U.S. businesses suffer because it entails a multilateral trade area that prevents the United States from making bilateral agreements; in his words, "the European Union, of course, was set up to take advantage of the United States."[308] And, as he later stressed, "the way they treat [the United States is] . . . hostile."[309]

He also has encouraged cracks in the EU's cohesion. He insisted that Theresa May's Brexit plan would "kill" a U.S.-UK trade deal because it would have retained customs rates between the UK and the EU, and he also reportedly suggested to Emmanuel Macron that France should leave the EU to get a better trade deal with the United States.[310] European leaders, who have long recognized that the strength of the European project depends to some degree on U.S. support, are now anxious that Trump will worsen the damage that it has suffered because of populist movements and economic stagnation across the continent.[311]

Nevertheless, Trump is right that the EU makes it more difficult for certain U.S. products to be sold there. Although tariff rates are not higher on average in the EU than in the United States, nontariff barriers, such as restrictions on agricultural sales because of stringent anti–genetically modified organism (GMO) public health laws, do cause problems.[312] The administration has largely replied with threats of tariffs. The president removed the EU's exemption on global steel and aluminum tariffs on May 31, 2018, and the EU responded with retaliatory tariffs on a wide variety of U.S. goods. Trump then threatened to place a 20 percent tariff on imported European cars.[313] This led to a July meeting between the president and European Commission President Jean-Claude Juncker, in which both agreed to start negotiations to reduce tariffs and pursue freer trade.[314]

New trade negotiations with the EU were announced in October 2018 and are currently underway.[315] Both sides face difficult questions about how to address EU barriers to U.S. agricultural exports and other nontariff hurdles, such as inspections regimes for products like electronics and government procurement restrictions. Because this negotiation is not in the context of a formal trade agreement, individual changes can be made incrementally. However, the EU does not want to include agriculture in its negotiations, and the steel and aluminum tariffs remain in place.[316] And, of course, all this strife in the U.S.-EU commercial relationship makes the European Union even less likely to join the United States in confronting China over its trade practices.

The most important dimension of the president's trade policies relates to China. Beijing's trade violations have been enduring and significant. China subsidizes state-owned industries, especially its steel and aluminum companies, and the resulting overcapacity dramatically undercuts metals prices.[317] It refuses to grant market access to U.S. and other firms across most of its economy.[318] It steals U.S. intellectual property and advanced technology. It forces foreign tech firms that want to operate and sell goods in the country to work directly with Chinese firms and give them access to their secrets.[319] It steals new technology from foreign firms inside China using cyber tools. According to cybersecurity firm CrowdStrike, China was "the most prolific nation-state threat actor during the first half of 2018" and "made targeted intrusion attempts against multiple sectors of the economy, including biotech, defense, mining, pharmaceutical, professional services, transportation, and more."[320] These attacks have continued into 2019.[321]

Trump was highly critical of these destructive Chinese trade practices before he became president. However, in his first year in office, he was much less bombastic and more willing to negotiate. Xi and Trump, in a meeting at the Mar-a-Lago resort, agreed to begin a dialogue on trade, and in May 2017 they announced an agreement that would give the United States slightly more market access, most notably for beef exports to China later that year.[322]

The following year, the president's trade actions toward China became more aggressive. In May 2018, the Trump administration, in negotiations with Beijing to address issues in U.S.-China trade, gave the Chinese a long list of demands, including to unilaterally reduce the trade deficit by $100 billion, end industrial subsidies for the Made in China 2025 program, and open up more of its economy to U.S. firms, without making concessions of its own.[323] The Chinese team refused, and talks stalled.

In July 2018, President Trump implemented a 25 percent tariff on $50 billion in Chinese imports and followed up with a 10 percent tariff on another $200 billion, with a threat to raise the rate to 25 percent on January 1, 2019.[324] China responded with retaliatory tariffs of its own.

At this writing, the United States and China are struggling to hammer out a trade deal that would reduce tariffs but is unlikely to result in meaningful changes to the Chinese economy.[325] These developments follow Trump's decision on February 24, 2019, to extend a March 2 deadline to escalate tariffs.[326] The agreement is reported to require Beijing to purchase large quantities of American agricultural and energy goods, including soybeans and $18 billion worth of liquefied natural gas, and to lower tariffs and other restrictions on farm, chemical, and auto products.[327] In exchange, the United States is considering dropping tariffs on at least $200 billion of the $250 billion worth of Chinese imports affected by American restrictions.[328]

Negotiators from both countries have been in talks to develop a mechanism to address complaints from U.S. companies, with U.S. tariffs being threatened should the talks fail to produce an agreement, although at the time of this writing it appears the details of such a mechanism have not been finalized.[329] The two sides have not come together on final terms, and prospects for a Trump-Xi summit are uncertain.[330]

Both sides have an incentive to make a deal. The Chinese economy's growth is slowing, and President Xi would like to have a stronger economic performance to build his legitimacy at home; President Trump wants a stronger U.S. economy and fewer Chinese restrictions on U.S. economic activity. But given its strategic priorities, China may not be willing to change its practices enough to justify President Trump's softening his stance.[331] China's failures to follow through on past promises to liberalize will also make reaching a final deal more difficult.[332]

Aside from the China trade dispute, which came about because of Beijing's malpractices, the trade crises with Canada, Mexico, South Korea, and the EU were driven primarily by the president's mistaken, long-held convictions about how trade works. Commercial differences between the United States and its partners in the advanced economies are not worth Trump's threats to dramatically reduce commerce. Moreover, the "fixes" he has so far negotiated have been similar to the agreements he scrapped or threatened to destroy: the new KORUS is virtually the same as before, and USMCA borrows much of its content from the TPP. However, the president's aggressive trade approach to China has the potential to be far more important in the long run in defending American equities than any of these other trade disputes.

*Trump Grade on Trade Policy: C*

# CONCLUSION
## Grade for Trump's Overall Foreign Policy

Making an overall judgment on the quality of the president's foreign policy is difficult for many reasons. It is necessary to separate his chaotic policy processes from the policies themselves. On many of the most important issues—China, North Korea, and Russia—the Trump administration scrambles to make sense of the president's public pronouncements, which are often made by tweet and are often as much a surprise to them as to the public.[333] Trump's own intelligence chiefs publicly contradict his views on Iran, North Korea, and the Islamic State in Syria, and he tells them to "go back to school."[334] He is increasingly at odds with Republican members of Congress and other officials in his own party. As the *New York Times'* Peter Baker puts it, "They think pulling out of Syria and Afghanistan would be a debacle. They think North Korea cannot be trusted. They think the Islamic State is still a threat to America. They think Russia is bad and NATO is good. The trouble is their president does not agree."[335]

Trump is said to refuse to read policy briefing papers before important meetings or decisions, or indeed at any other time.[336] He has contempt for diplomacy and the officers who conduct it.[337] While the world turns and important international issues arise, the president spends his time concentrating on a nonexistent threat to the U.S. southern border and watching cable news broadcasts. In short, President Trump takes no advantage of the enormous analytical capabilities of the only superpower on earth, and instead, as America's pilot, usually flies without either navigational aids or clear destinations. And he seems to enjoy the policy turbulence that so distresses most of the media. *On issues of policy process, President Trump gets an F.*

Then there are the president's character and personal qualities. As jurist Robert Ingersoll said when referring to Abraham Lincoln's integrity, "Most people can bear adversity. But if you wish to know what a man really is, give him power."[338] In that context, finding any attractive feature of Donald Trump's personality is difficult. He lies; his word is worthless.[339] He takes credit for ideas that were first introduced centuries ago.[340] His views on women and people of color are a disgrace.[341] He brags to Boy Scouts and others about his tawdry private life.[342] He bullies.[343] He disparages and has no empathy for those less fortunate than himself.[344] He makes fun of the disabled.[345] He slurs the reputations of those who have worked loyally for him.[346] In sum, there apparently are no better angels in the president's character. This matters in foreign affairs because other governments assess the personal behavior and character of the president and his consequent reliability as an interlocutor and decision-maker. *On issues of character, President Trump gets an F.*

Next is the question of American values. Trump is a president who persistently attempts to deceive the people of the United States about the substance of his policies; who undermines U.S. democratic institutions—the judiciary, law enforcement and especially the FBI, Congress, the media, and career government workers (the so-called deep state)—which weakens American capacity to project power abroad; who peddles fear and division as domestic political strategies; and who globally besmirches America's aspiration, since its founding, to be a democratic beacon on the hill.[347] *On the promotion of U.S. values at home and abroad, President Trump gets an F.*

Whether a given policy is sensible is irrelevant if its implementation is incompetent. And that implementation is usually carried out by officials who never set foot in Trump's Oval Office. The many unfilled senior policy positions at the State and Defense Departments unquestionably weaken such implementation.[348] Moreover, it is too early to make a final judgment regarding how effective the administration's policy implementation will be over time. Yet even with this caveat, it is difficult at this writing to be confident that the weak bureaucracy that characterizes the Trump presidency in foreign affairs will be capable of sustained skillful policy implementation. *On the implementation of his policies, President Trump gets a D.*

To assign the president an overall grade, it is also necessary to evaluate the psychological effects of Trump's combative approach to America's European and Asian allies and closest friends. The United States cannot thrive in the world and manifest sufficient power projection without strong alliances, which U.S. presidents from both political parties since Harry S. Truman have worked to build over seven decades. These intimate and long-standing diplomatic, economic, and security networks have been, along with the domestic strength and vitality of the United States, the enduring foundations of U.S. foreign policy. Much depends on allies' confidence in the reliability of U.S. resolve and treaty guarantees.

In this regard, words can be consequential actions. Rhetoric by the American president matters—it affects U.S. credibility among alliance members; it affects the allied sense of U.S. steadfastness; and it affects the strength and credibility of deterrence. These central issues are nearly as old as America's alliances. Charles de Gaulle became so convinced that the United States could not be depended on to persuasively threaten to use its nuclear weapons and thus risk New York to save Paris that France developed its own nuclear deterrent.[349] Each previous president since the 1950s has sought, more or less successfully, to persuade allies that President de Gaulle was mistaken.

Today, it is not the French president but Trump who has raised this issue again. With his repeated comments, he has dangerously questioned U.S. commitments to these indispensable U.S. alliances, from the Baltic nations through Europe to South Korea and Japan, and the leaders and populations of all these countries increasingly doubt the resilience and reliability of the United States. He has increased the likelihood of a failure of deterrence, encouraged adversaries to take greater risks, and brought war closer. President de Gaulle would feel vindicated. *On his approach to U.S. alliances and deterrence, President Trump gets an F.*

All the chaos generated by this flawed president does produce actual policies, the substance of which in many cases is likely to be more consequential than the ways by which the policies arrived and the character of the man who formulated them.[350] On the one hand, the Trump administration has made an extraordinary contribution to U.S. security by contesting the complacent and dangerous shibboleths regarding the rise of China, which had been developed by its predecessors in the previous nearly two decades. On the other hand, Trump's views on climate change will represent crucial challenges for his successors for decades to come.

*The grades for President Trump's foreign policies just past the halfway point in his term are: China (B+), North Korea (B), Syria (B+), Saudi Arabia (B+), Israel (B), Iran (C), Afghanistan (B+), India (B+), Venezuela (B+), and trade (C); against his grades for climate (F), European security (D), Russia (F), policy process (F), character (F), American values (F), U.S. alliances and deterrence (F), and policy implementation (D).*

This report, heavily influenced by the president's realistic approaches to China and the greater Middle East, gives him an *overall foreign policy grade of D+*, a substantially higher mark for his foreign policies than found on the Sunday talk shows, in the editorial pages of the *New York Times* and *Washington Post*, or among many U.S. national security experts.

In view of Trump's record in office and in the decades before, it is impossible to know whether Trump policies today will be Trump policies tomorrow, or whether his populist approach to America's role in the world will endure after his presidency.[351] Pundits argue that Trump's destructive populism will not leave the Oval Office when he does, but they are guessing.[352] There is no definitive way to make such judgments (one remembers Jacksonianism and its remedial aftermath), and the policies and character of his immediate successor will obviously be crucial in determining the future of American foreign policy.[353] But given the stakes involved, there are reasons to worry.

For instance, the president and his colleagues might continue to react strongly and effectively to the problematic elements in the rise of China and build up U.S. power projection into Asia; or, in the context of a trade deal, Trump might decide Xi Jinping is America's greatest friend, say so publicly, and thus alarm U.S. Asian allies and weaken deterrence. Because of his setbacks elsewhere, he might accept cosmetic trade moves by China and declare such an agreement a triumphant success. Trump might make further spontaneous and uninformed concessions to North Korea without concrete steps by Kim to denuclearize, in order to describe his policies as successful. Or, rather than take a step-by-step approach, he might suddenly return to his "fire and fury" rhetoric and demand North Korea's agreement at the outset to verifiably destroy all its nuclear weapons. He might make private commitments to Vladimir Putin that embolden Moscow to try more aggressively, perhaps even with much more direct use of force, to bring Ukraine again securely within Russia's orbit. Trump might begin a U.S. military withdrawal from Europe. He might cause a prolonged crisis among America's alliances by seeking to charge 150 percent of the cost of stationing U.S. troops in those nations.[354] He might pursue unsound trade policies until they contribute to a global economic downturn. He might use military force against Venezuela. With no diplomatic strategy, he might lurch into a war with Iran.[355]

Unfortunately for America, given Donald J. Trump's enduring lack of character, his refusal to learn, his uneducated biases, the chaotic and dysfunctional way that he runs the government, and the diminishing quality of his senior advisors, the president's foreign policy grade is unlikely to improve in the years ahead and could get much worse. But as Alexander Pope observed, "Hope springs eternal in the human breast."[356]

# ENDNOTES

1.  Indeed, one is reminded of Edgar Wilson "Bill" Nye's quip that "Wagner's music is better than it sounds." Harriet Elinor Smith, ed., *Autobiography of Mark Twain, Volume 1* (Berkeley: University of California Press, 2010), 288.

2.  Conversation with the author.

3.  Glenn Kessler et al., "In 773 Days, President Trump Has Made 9,014 False or Misleading Claims," *Washington Post*, updated March 3, 2019, http://washingtonpost.com/graphics /politics/trump-claims-database.

4.  For example, when Trump unveiled his plan to withdraw U.S. troops from Syria, he did not consult General Joseph Votel, commander of U.S. Central Command, who confirmed that he "was not aware of the specific announcement." See Rebecca Kheel, "Top General Says He Wasn't Consulted Before Trump Announced Syria Withdrawal," *Hill*, February 5, 2019, http://thehill.com/policy/defense/428509-top-general-says-he -wasnt-consulted-before-trump-announced-syria-withdrawal.

5.  See Robert Kagan, "Springtime for Strongmen," *Foreign Policy*, Winter 2019, http:// foreignpolicy.com/gt-essay/springtime-for-strongmen-authoritarian-leaders-china -russia-north-korea-venezuela-turkey; and Griff Witte et al., "Around the Globe, Trump's Style Is Inspiring Imitators and Unleashing Dark Impulses," *Washington Post*, January 22, 2019, http://washingtonpost.com/world/europe/around-the-globe-trumps -style-is-inspiring-imitators-and-unleashing-dark-impulses/2019/01/22/ebd15952 -1366-11e9-ab79-30cd4f7926f2_story.html.

6.  Lily Kuo, "'Divide and Conquer': China Puts the Pressure on U.S. Allies," *Guardian*, February 2, 2019, http://theguardian.com/world/2019/feb/02/divide-and-conquer-china -puts-the-pressure-on-us-allies.

7.  Richard Wike et al., "Trump's International Ratings Remain Low, Especially Among Key Allies," Pew Research Center, October 1, 2018, http://pewglobal.org/2018/10/01 /trumps-international-ratings-remain-low-especially-among-key-allies; and Jeffrey Stacey, "U.S. Foreign Policy in Free Fall," *National Interest*, January 24, 2019, http:// nationalinterest.org/feature/us-foreign-policy-free-fall-42387.

8.  Jacob Poushter and Christine Huang, "Climate Change Still Seen as the Top Global Threat, but Cyberattacks a Rising Concern," Pew Research Center, February 10, 2019, http://pewglobal.org/2019/02/10/climate-change-still-seen-as-the-top-global-threat -but-cyberattacks-a-rising-concern.

9. Among the best books that see few or no redeeming virtues in Trump's foreign policy are Bob Woodward, *Fear: Trump in the White House* (New York: Simon and Schuster, 2018); Robert Kagan, *The Jungle Grows Back: America and Our Imperiled World* (New York: Alfred A. Knopf, 2018); Ivo H. Daalder and James M. Lindsay, *The Empty Throne: America's Abdication of Global Leadership* (New York: PublicAffairs, 2018); and Kori Schake, *America vs the West: Can the Liberal World Order Be Preserved?* (North Sydney: Penguin Random House Australia, 2018). Articles giving the president some credit for his foreign policy are Nahal Toosi, "Trump's Skeptics Pondering Whether He Deserves More Credit," *Politico*, February 5, 2019, http://politico.com/story/2019/02/05/trump -foreign-policy-afghanistan-1145766; Daniel Fried, "Two Years of the Trump Foreign Policy: The Good, the Bad, and the Worst," *New Atlanticist* (blog), Atlantic Council, January 17, 2019, http://atlanticcouncil.org/blogs/new-atlanticist/two-years-of-the -trump-foreign-policy-the-good-the-bad-and-the-worst; and Randall Schweller, "Three Cheers for Trump's Foreign Policy: What the Establishment Misses," *Foreign Affairs*, September/October 2018, http://foreignaffairs.com/articles/world/2018-08-13/three -cheers-trumps-foreign-policy.

10. See Kelly Magsamen and Michael Fuchs, "Destroying the Foundations of U.S. Foreign Policy," Center for American Progress, June 28, 2018, http://americanprogress.org /issues/security/reports/2018/06/28/452913/destroying-foundations-u-s-foreign -policy.

11. Stephen M. Walt, "Why Trump Is Getting Away With Foreign-Policy Insanity," *Foreign Policy*, July 18, 2018, http://foreignpolicy.com/2018/07/18/why-trump-is-getting-away -with-foreign-policy-insanity.

12. "On Donald Trump's Foreign Policy, There Is No Method to His Apparent Madness," editorial, *USA Today*, June 3, 2018, http://usatoday.com/story/opinion/2018/06/03 /donald-trump-foreign-policy-no-method-his-madness-editorials-debates/661329002.

13. "Under Mr. Trump, America Surrenders," editorial, *New York Times*, October 16, 2017, http://nytimes.com/2017/10/16/opinion/trump-america-international-surrender.html.

14. See Michael Mandelbaum, "The New Containment: Handling Russia, China, and Iran," *Foreign Affairs*, March/April 2019, http://foreignaffairs.com/articles/china/2019-02-12 /new-containment. Richard Haass makes this point in *A World in Disarray*, written before Trump took office. See Haass, *A World in Disarray: American Foreign Policy and the Crisis of the Old Order* (New York: Penguin Books, 2017).

15. Henry Kissinger, "How the Enlightenment Ends," *Atlantic*, June 2018, http://theatlantic .com/magazine/archive/2018/06/henry-kissinger-ai-could-mean-the-end-of-human -history/559124.

16. T. S. Eliot, "Journey of the Magi," *Ariel Poems* (London: Faber and Faber Ltd., 2014).

17. Colin Kahl and Hal Brands, "Trump's Grand Strategic Train Wreck," *Foreign Policy*, January 31, 2017, http://foreignpolicy.com/2017/01/31/trumps-grand-strategic-train -wreck.

18. For example, before his first summit with Kim Jong-un in June 2018, President Trump stated, "I don't think I have to prepare very much. It's about the attitude. It's about willingness to get things done." See John Wagner, "'It's About the Attitude': Trump Says He Doesn't Have to Prepare Much for His Summit With North Korea's Leader,"

*Washington Post*, June 7, 2018, http://washingtonpost.com/politics/its-about-the
-attitude-trump-says-he-doesnt-have-to-prepare-much-for-his-summit-with-north
-koreas-leader/2018/06/07/2af3ec7e-6a6d-11e8-9e38-24e693b38637_story.html.

19.  There is a lively debate concerning whether Trump has a grand strategy. See Hal Brands,
     *American Grand Strategy in the Age of Trump* (Washington, DC: Brookings Institution
     Press, 2018); Gabriel Schoenfeld, "Does Trump Have a Grand Strategy for Foreign
     Policy? Dream On," *USA Today*, December 27, 2017, http://usatoday.com/story
     /opinion/2017/12/27/donald-trump-grand-strategy-foreign-policy-dream-gabriel
     -schoenfeld-column/981699001; Peter Dombrowski and Simon Reich, "Does Donald
     Trump Have a Grand Strategy?," *International Affairs* 93, no. 5 (2017): 1013–1037,
     http://doi.org/10.1093/ia/iix161; Rebecca Friedman Lissner and Micah Zenko, "There
     Is No Trump Doctrine, and There Will Never Be One," *Foreign Policy*, July 21, 2017,
     http://foreignpolicy.com/2017/07/21/there-is-no-trump-doctrine-and-there-will-never
     -be-one-grand-strategy; Daniel Wagner, "Trump's Grand Strategy in Foreign Policy,"
     *International Policy Digest*, July 8, 2018, http://intpolicydigest.org/2018/07/08/trump
     -s-grand-strategy-in-foreign-policy; Brahma Chellaney, "Trump's Grand Strategy,"
     *Project Syndicate*, July 30, 2018, http://project-syndicate.org/commentary/trump-grand
     -strategy-china-us-decline-by-brahma-chellaney-2018-07; Eliot A. Cohen, "America's
     Long Goodbye: The Real Crisis of the Trump Era," *Foreign Affairs*, January/February
     2019, http://foreignaffairs.com/articles/united-states/long-term-disaster-trump-foreign
     -policy; Walter Russell Mead, "Trump Is No 'Isolationist,'" *Wall Street Journal*, October
     22, 2018, http://wsj.com/articles/trump-is-no-isolationist-1540250070; Edoardo
     Baldaro and Matteo Dian, "Trump's Grand Strategy and the Post-American World
     Order," *Interdisciplinary Political Studies* 4, no. 1 (2018): 17–45, http://siba-ese
     .unisalento.it/index.php/idps/article/view/19338; and Ross Douthat, "The Trump
     Doctrine," *New York Times*, January 29, 2019, http://nytimes.com/2019/01/29/opinion
     /trump-doctrine-venezuela-afghanistan.html. See also Benjamin H. Friedman and Justin
     Logan, "Why Washington Doesn't Debate Grand Strategy," *Strategic Studies Quarterly*
     10, no. 4 (Winter 2016): 14–45, http://airuniversity.af.edu/Portals/10/SSQ/documents
     /Volume-10_Issue-4/Friedman.pdf.

20.  It is true that Trump has had the same views regarding alliances, trade, and
     dictatorships versus democracies for three decades, but these effusions hardly qualify
     as grand strategy.

21.  Robert A. Caro, *The Years of Lyndon Johnson*, 4 vols. (New York: Alfred A. Knopf,
     1982–2012).

22.  Distinguished historian Niall Ferguson observes that virtually the entire foreign policy
     establishment has portrayed Trump, in varying shades, as a maniacal populist. See
     Ferguson, "A Terrible, Horrible, No Good, Very Bad President Builds an Empire,"
     *Boston Globe*, June 11, 2018, http://bostonglobe.com/opinion/2018/06/11/terrible
     -horrible-good-very-bad-president-builds-empire/quXTOXsKAIJIUbHwEnTkOO
     /story.html.

23.  Fox News Sunday (@FoxNewsSunday), "President Trump rates his job performance
     compared to past presidents. He tells Chris, 'I would give myself an A+.'
     #POTUSonFNS," Twitter, November 18, 2018, 7:14 a.m., http://twitter.com
     /FoxNewsSunday/status/1064175137593978881; and Peter Baker and Maggie
     Haberman, "Trump, Defending His Mental Fitness, Says He's a 'Very Stable Genius,'"

*New York Times*, January 6, 2018, http://nytimes.com/2018/01/06/us/politics/trump
-genius-mental-health.html.

24. Steven Shepard, "Trump Grades Himself an A+. Voters Don't Agree," *Politico*, January
25, 2019, http://politico.com/story/2019/01/25/trump-voters-report-card-1124761.
On the issue of foreign relations, 27 percent gave him an A or a B, 13 percent gave a C,
and 17 percent didn't know or had no opinion.

25. I am in debt to Philip Zelikow for pointing this out in a private exchange.

26. Trump could intend to pressure the allies to increase their defense spending and
capabilities to bolster transatlantic deterrence, or he could intend to gradually weaken
the U.S. treaty commitment to the North Atlantic Treaty Organization and thus to
separate the United States from Europe.

27. To cite just two other familiar examples, the Franklin D. Roosevelt administration could
not imagine that Japan would attack Pearl Harbor, in December 1941; and Pharaoh
clearly did not sufficiently take into account Moses's strategic and tactical assets, in
this case his God, as he led the Israelites out of captivity in Egypt and into the land of
Canaan. The Egyptian intelligence community's failure regarding collection, collation,
evaluation, analysis, integration, and interpretation reportedly cost Pharaoh his entire
army and all its equipment in the Red Sea.

28. Bill Clinton and Jiang Zemin, "China-U.S. Joint Statement," Washington, DC, October
29, 1997, http://www.china-embassy.org/eng/zmgx/zywj/t36259.htm.

29. George W. Bush and Jiang Zemin, "U.S., China Stand Against Terrorism" (joint press
conference, Shanghai, October 19, 2001), U.S. Department of State, http:// 2001-2009
.state.gov/s/ct/rls/rm/2001/5461.htm.

30. Barack Obama and Xi Jinping, "Remarks in Joint Press Conference" (joint
press conference, Washington, DC, September 25, 2015), White House, http://
obamawhitehouse.archives.gov/the-press-office/2015/09/25/remarks-president-obama
-and-president-xi-peoples-republic-china-joint.

31. Kuo, "'Divide and Conquer'"; Robert D. Blackwill and Ashley J. Tellis, *Revising U.S.
Grand Strategy Toward China* (New York: Council on Foreign Relations, 2015), http://
cfr.org/report/revising-us-grand-strategy-toward-china; Robert D. Blackwill and
Jennifer M. Harris, *War by Other Means: Geoeconomics and Statecraft* (Cambridge,
MA: Harvard University Press, 2016): 93–151; and Robert D. Blackwill, "Indo-Pacific
Strategy in an Era of Geoeconomics" (speech, Tokyo, July 31, 2018), http://cfrd8-files
.cfr.org/sites/default/files/pdf/8-20%20Tokyo%20Presentation.pdf. In their book,
Blackwill and Harris define geoeconomics as "the use of economic instruments to
promote and defend national interests and to produce beneficial geopolitical results,
and the effects of other nations' economic actions on a country's geopolitical goals"
(9). See also Commission on the Theft of American Intellectual Property, *Update to the
IP Commission Report: The Theft of American Intellectual Property; Reassessments of the
Challenge and United States Policy* (Washington: National Bureau of Asian Research,
2017), http://ipcommission.org/report/IP_Commission_Report_Update_2017.pdf;
Gerry Shih, "Xi Offers Promises and Threats as He Calls China's Unification With
Taiwan Inevitable," *Washington Post*, January 2, 2019, http://washingtonpost.com
/world/asia_pacific/xi-offers-promises-and-threats-as-he-calls-chinas-unification-with
-taiwan-inevitable/2019/01/02/85ae5ece-0e82-11e9-92b8-6dd99e2d80e1_story.html;

"Advance Policy Questions for Admiral Philip Davidson, USN, Expected Nominee for Commander, U.S. Pacific Command," April 17, 2018, U.S. Senate Committee on Armed Services, http://armed-services.senate.gov/imo/media/doc/Davidson_APQs _04-17-18.pdf; Robert D. Blackwill and Kurt M. Campbell, *Xi Jinping on the Global Stage* (New York: Council on Foreign Relations, 2016), http://cfr.org/report/xi-jinping -global-stage; "China," in *World Report 2019*, Human Rights Watch, http://hrw.org /world-report/2019/country-chapters/china-and-tibet; and Anne Applebaum, "'Never Again?' It's Already Happening.," *Washington Post*, February 15, 2019, http:// washingtonpost.com/opinions/global-opinions/the-west-ignored-crimes-against -humanity-in-the-1930s-its-happening-again-now/2019/02/15/d17d4998-3130-11e9 -813a-0ab2f17e305b_story.html.

32.   Lee Kuan Yew, quoted in Graham Allison and Robert Blackwill, *Lee Kuan Yew: The Grand Master's Insights on China, the United States, and the World* (Cambridge, MA: MIT Press, 2013): 2.

33.   For example, David Brooks of the *New York Times* now describes China as "an existential threat for the 21st century." See Brooks, "How China Brings Us Together," *New York Times*, February 14, 2019, http://nytimes.com/2019/02/14/opinion/china -economy.html.

34.   Robert D. Blackwill and Theodore Rappleye, "Trump's Five Mistaken Reasons for Withdrawing From the Trans-Pacific Partnership," *Foreign Policy*, June 22, 2017, http:// foreignpolicy.com/2017/06/22/trumps-five-mistaken-reasons-for-withdrawing-from -the-trans-pacific-partnership-china-trade-economics.

35.   "National Security Strategy of the United States of America," White House, December 18, 2017, 21, 46, http://whitehouse.gov/wp-content/uploads/2017/12/NSS-Final-12 -18-2017-0905.pdf.

36.   "Summary of the 2018 National Defense Strategy of the United States: Sharpening the American Military's Competitive Edge," Department of Defense, 2018, 1, http:// dod.defense.gov/Portals/1/Documents/pubs/2018-National-Defense-Strategy -Summary.pdf.

37.   Mike Pence, "Remarks by Vice President Pence on the Administration's Policy Toward China" (speech, Washington, DC, October 4, 2018), http://whitehouse.gov/briefings -statements/remarks-vice-president-pence-administrations-policy-toward-china.

38.   Exec. Order No. 13859, 84 Fed. Reg. 3967 (Feb. 14, 2019), http://govinfo.gov/content /pkg/FR-2019-02-14/pdf/2019-02544.pdf.

39.   Jim Tankersley and Keith Bradsher, "Trump Hits China With Tariffs on $200 Billion in Goods, Escalating Trade War," *New York Times*, September 17, 2018, http://nytimes .com/2018/09/17/us/politics/trump-china-tariffs-trade.html.

40.   Paul Wiseman and Catherine Lucey, "Trump Extends China Tariff Deadline, Cites Progress in Talks," Associated Press, February 24, 2019, http://apnews.com /0104a56ab495461f86cf4883b8d69ee7; Kevin Breuninger and Javier David, "U.S. Will Hold Off on Raising China Tariffs to 25% as Trump and Xi Agree to a 90-Day Trade Truce," CNBC, December 3, 2018, http://cnbc.com/2018/12/01/us-china -wont-impose-additional-tariffs-after-january-1-report.html.

41.   For an explanation of Trump's mistaken assumptions about trade, see Martin Feldstein,

"Inconvenient Truths About the U.S. Trade Deficit," *Project Syndicate*, April 25, 2017, http://nber.org/feldstein/projectsyndicateapr252017.html.

42. See, for example, Kayla Tausche and Michael Sheetz, "China Offers 6-Year Import Boost in Trade Talks With U.S.: Sources," CNBC, January 18, 2019, http://cnbc.com/2019/01/18/china-to-offer-path-to-eliminate-trade-imbalance-with-us-report.html.

43. Kelly Olsen, "China Respects Others' Trade Secrets—Unless It Wants Something, Experts Say," CNBC, October 4, 2018, http://cnbc.com/2018/10/04/trade-secret-protection-remains-a-challenge-in-china-even-experts.html.

44. See Julia Horowitz, "How Huawei's CFO Ended Up in a Canadian Jail Cell," CNN, December 11, 2018, http://cnn.com/2018/12/11/business/huawei-cfo-arrest-details/index.html; David Sanger, Julian E. Barnes, Raymond Zhong, and Mark Santora, "In 5G Race With China, U.S. Pushes Allies to Fight Huawei," *New York Times*, January 26, 2018, http://nytimes.com/2019/01/26/us/politics/huawei-china-us-5g-technology.html; and Ellen Nakashima and Devlin Barrett, "Justice Department Charges Huawei With Fraud, Ratcheting Up U.S.-China Tensions," *Washington Post*, http://washingtonpost.com/world/national-security/justice-dept-charges-huawei-with-fraud-ratcheting-up-us-china-tensions/2019/01/28/70a7f550-2320-11e9-81fd-b7b05d5bed90_story.html.

45. Julian E. Barnes, "Administration Readies Order to Keep China Out of Wireless Networks," *New York Times*, February 12, 2019, http://nytimes.com/2019/02/12/us/politics/trump-china-wireless-networks.html.

46. Claire Ballentine, "U.S. Lifts Ban That Kept ZTE From Doing Business With American Suppliers," *New York Times*, July 13, 2018, http://nytimes.com/2018/07/13/business/zte-ban-trump.html.

47. See "Status of the Navy," December 16, 2016, http://web.archive.org/web/20161231004411/http://navy.mil/navydata/nav_legacy.asp?id=146; and "Status of the Navy," January 17, 2019, http://web.archive.org/web/20190118025156/http://navy.mil/navydata/nav_legacy.asp?id=146.

48. Dean Cheng, "Wanted: A Strategy to Limit China's Grand Plans for the South China Sea," Heritage Foundation, January 31, 2018, http://heritage.org/homeland-security/commentary/wanted-strategy-limit-chinas-grand-plans-the-south-china-sea; Zack Cooper and Gregory Poling, "America's Freedom of Navigation Operations Are Lost at Sea," *Foreign Policy*, January 8, 2019, http://foreignpolicy.com/2019/01/08/americas-freedom-of-navigation-operations-are-lost-at-sea; and Sun Tian, "China Strongly Dissatisfied by U.S. Warships Entering South China Sea," *ECNS*, February 11, 2019, http://www.ecns.cn/news/politics/2019-02-11/detail-ifzekwei6640415.shtml.

49. Tian, "China Strongly Dissatisfied by U.S. Warships Entering South China Sea."

50. *The Military and Security Challenges and Posture in the Indo-Pacific Region, Before the House Armed Services Comm.*, 115th Cong. (2018) (statement of Admiral Harry Harris Jr., U.S. Navy, Commander, U.S. Pacific Command), http://docs.house.gov/meetings/AS/AS00/20180214/106847/HHRG-115-AS00-Wstate-HarrisJrH-20180214.pdf.

51. "Department of the Navy Strategic Roadmap for Unmanned Systems (Short Version)," http://assets.documentcloud.org/documents/4486563/Navy-UxS-Roadmap-Summary

.pdf; and Richard Scott, "LRASM Completes Second Dual-Missile Flight Test," *Jane's 360* (blog), IHS Markit, May 24, 2018, http://janes.com/article/80301/lrasm-completes -second-dual-missile-flight-test.

52. *The Military and Security Challenges and Posture in the Indo-Pacific Region*, 33–35.

53. Franz-Stefan Gady, "U.S., Japan Kick Off Military Exercise Involving 57,000 Personnel," *Diplomat*, October 30, 2018, http://thediplomat.com/2018/10/us-japan -kick-off-military-exercise-involving-57000-personnel.

54. Alastair Gale and Chieko Tsuneoka, "Japan Heeds Trump's Call With American-Made Defense Spending Spree," *Wall Street Journal*, December 18, 2018, http://wsj.com /articles/japan-to-buy-105-more-f-35-fighters-11545098435.

55. Colin Packham, "Australia, United States Begin Their Biggest Military Exercise," Reuters, June 29, 2017, http://reuters.com/article/us-australia-usa-military -idUSKBN19K0ID.

56. Scott Neuman, "In Military Name Change, U.S. Pacific Command Becomes U.S. Indo-Pacific Command," NPR, May 31, 2018, http://npr.org/sections/thetwo-way /2018/05/31/615722120/in-military-name-change-u-s-pacific-command-becomes -u-s-indo-pacific-command; and Maria Abi-Habib, "U.S. and India, Wary of China, Agree to Strengthen Military Ties," *New York Times*, September 6, 2018, http://nytimes .com/2018/09/06/world/asia/us-india-military-agreement.html.

57. Office of the Spokesperson, "U.S. Security Cooperation in the Indo-Pacific Region: Fact Sheet," U.S. Department of State, August 4, 2018, http://state.gov/r/pa/prs/ps /2018/08/284927.htm.

58. Mike Pence, "Remarks by Vice President Pence at the 2018 APEC CEO Summit" (speech, Port Moresby, Papua New Guinea, November 16, 2018), http://whitehouse .gov/briefings-statements/remarks-vice-president-pence-2018-apec-ceo-summit-port -moresby-papua-new-guinea.

59. See Blackwill, "Indo-Pacific Strategy in an Era of Geoeconomics."

60. See Nadege Rolland, "Reports of Belt and Road's Death Are Greatly Exaggerated," *Foreign Affairs*, January 29, 2019, http://foreignaffairs.com/articles/china/2019-01-29 /reports-belt-and-roads-death-are-greatly-exaggerated.

61. Mike Pompeo, "Remarks on 'America's Indo-Pacific Vision'" (speech, Washington, DC, July 30, 2018), http://state.gov/secretary/remarks/2018/07/284722.html. For a low estimate, see "MERICS Belt and Road Tracker," Mercator Institute for China Studies, http://merics.org/en/bri-tracker; for a high estimate, see Cecilia Joy-Perez and Derek Scissors, "The Chinese State Funds Belt and Road but Does Not Have Trillions to Spare," American Enterprise Institute, March 2018, http://aei.org/wp-content/uploads /2018/03/BRI.pdf.

62. The Build Act, signed into law in October 2018, created the U.S. International Development Finance Corporation to enlarge and streamline development investment projects. The Trump administration supported this legislation as it was being drafted. See Pompeo, "Remarks on 'America's Indo-Pacific Vision'"; and Daniel F. Runde and Romina Bandura, "The Build Act Has Passed: What's Next?," Center for Strategic and International Studies, October 12, 2018, http://csis.org/analysis/build-act-has-passed -whats-next.

63. "Joint Statement of the Governments of the United States of America, Australia, and Japan," November 17, 2018, http://whitehouse.gov/briefings-statements/joint-statement-governments-united-states-america-australia-japan.

64. See also James Dobbins, Howard J. Schatz, and Ali Wyne, *Russia Is a Rogue, Not a Peer; China Is a Peer, Not a Rogue: Different Challenges, Different Responses* (Santa Monica, CA: RAND Corporation, 2018), http://rand.org/pubs/perspectives/PE310.html. The authors note that China's geoeconomic challenge is now much stronger than the military threat it poses.

65. The classic work on the characteristics of Chinese diplomacy is Henry Kissinger, *On China* (New York: Penguin, 2011). See also Kevin Rudd's thoughtful *U.S.-China 21: The Future of U.S.-China Relations Under Xi Jinping* (Cambridge, MA: Belfer Center for Science and International Affairs, 2015).

66. See Graham Allison, *Destined for War: Can America and China Escape Thucydides's Trap?* (New York: Houghton Mifflin Harcourt, 2017); Derek Grossman, "No Smiles Across the Taiwan Strait," *Foreign Policy*, January 9, 2019, http://foreignpolicy.com/2019/01/07/no-smiles-across-the-taiwan-strait; Michael Mazza, "Is a Storm Brewing in the Taiwan Strait?," *Foreign Affairs*, July 27, 2018, http://foreignaffairs.com/articles/asia/2018-07-27/storm-brewing-taiwan-strait; Chris Buckley and Chris Horton, "Xi Jinping Warns Taiwan That Unification Is the Goal and Force Is an Option," *New York Times*, January 1, 2019, http://nytimes.com/2019/01/01/world/asia/xi-jinping-taiwan-china.html; and John Pomfret, "China's Xi Jinping Is Growing Impatient With Taiwan, Adding to Tensions With U.S.," *Washington Post*, February 18, 2019, http://washingtonpost.com/opinions/2019/02/18/chinas-xi-jinping-is-growing-impatient-with-taiwan-adding-tensions-with-united-states. See also Eric Heginbotham and Rajan Menon, "Taiwan's Balancing Act," *National Interest*, February 11, 2019, http://nationalinterest.org/feature/taiwans-balancing-act-44247.

67. The list of demands the Trump administration presented to China before it imposed tariffs, which bid Beijing to unilaterally cut its trade surplus with the United States by $100 billion and to give up its Made in China 2025 initiative to develop more advanced technology indigenously, is a case in point. See the draft framework, "Balancing the Trade Relationship Between the United States of America and the People's Republic of China," via Martin Wolf, "Donald Trump Declares Trade War on China," *Financial Times*, May 8, 2018, http://xqdoc.imedao.com/16329fa0c8b2da913fc9058b.pdf.

68. This section is reprinted from Robert D. Blackwill, "Managing the U.S.-China Great Power Relationship" (presentation, World Cultural Forum, Shanghai, June 18, 2014), http://belfercenter.org/publication/managing-us-china-great-power-relationship. At the time, Blackwill was a member of the board and the international council of the Belfer Center for Science and International Affairs.

69. See Jean-Luc Saaman, "Confronting the Flaws in America's Indo-Pacific Strategy," *War on the Rocks*, February 11, 2019, http://warontherocks.com/2019/02/confronting-the-flaws-in-americas-indo-pacific-strategy.

70. Kissinger, *On China*, 236.

71. See Richard Armitage and Joseph Nye, *More Important Than Ever: Renewing the U.S.-Japan Alliance for the 21st Century* (Washington, DC: Center for Strategic and International Studies, 2018), http://csis-prod.s3.amazonaws.com/s3fs-public

/publication/181011_MorethanEver.pdf; James L. Schoff, *Uncommon Alliance for the Common Good: The United States and Japan After the Cold War* (Washington, DC: Carnegie Endowment for International Peace, 2017), http://carnegieendowment.org /2017/01/23/uncommon-alliance-for-common-good-united-states-and-japan-after -cold-war-pub-67742; and Seth Crospey and Jun Isomura, "The U.S.-Japan Alliance: Significance and Role," Hudson Institute, April 2, 2018, http://hudson.org/research /14233-the-u-s-japan-alliance-significance-and-role.

72.  Robert Zoellick, "Whither China? From Membership to Responsibility" (speech, New York, September 21, 2005), http://ncuscr.org/sites/default/files/migration/Zoellick _remarks_notes06_winter_spring.pdf. Zoellick is often misquoted. He expressed an aspiration regarding China's policy, not an assertion that Beijing had already become a "responsible stakeholder."

73.  George Soros, quoted in Adam Taylor, "The Most Notable Rebuke of China at Davos Didn't Come From a Trump Ally. It Came From George Soros," *Washington Post*, January 25, 2019, http://washingtonpost.com/world/2019/01/25/most-notable-rebuke -china-davos-didnt-come-trump-ally-it-came-george-soros.

74.  Donald J. Trump (@realDonaldTrump), "The concept of global warming was created by and for the Chinese in order to make U.S. manufacturing non-competitive.," Twitter, November 6, 2012, 11:15 a.m., http://twitter.com/realdonaldtrump/status /265895292191248385; Donald J. Trump (@realDonaldTrump), "We should be focused on magnificently clean and healthy air and not distracted by the expensive hoax that is global warming!" Twitter, December 6, 2013, 7:38 a.m., http://twitter .com/realdonaldtrump/status/408983789830815744; Donald J. Trump (@ realDonaldTrump), "Give me clean, beautiful and healthy air - not the same old climate change (global warming) bullshit! I am tired of hearing this nonsense.," Twitter, January 28, 2014, 10:44 p.m., http://twitter.com/realdonaldtrump/status /428418323660165120; Donald J. Trump, quoted in Josh Dawsey, Philip Rucker, Brady Dennis, and Chris Mooney, "Trump on Climate Change: 'People Like Myself, We Have Very High Levels of Intelligence but We're Not Necessarily Such Believers,'" *Washington Post*, November 27, 2018, http://washingtonpost.com/politics/trump -on-climate-change-people-like-myself-we-have-very-high-levels-of-intelligence -but-were-not-necessarily-such-believers/2018/11/27/722f0184-f27e-11e8-aeea -b85fd44449f5_story.html.

75.  Donald J. Trump (@realDonaldTrump), "In the beautiful Midwest, windchill temperatures are reaching minus 60 degrees, the coldest ever recorded. In coming days, expected to get even colder. People can't last outside even for minutes. What the hell is going on with Global Waming? Please come back fast, we need you!," Twitter, January 28, 2019, 6:28 p.m., http://twitter.com/realDonaldTrump/status /1090074254010404864.

76.  John Gage, "Trump's State of the Union Was the Longest Since Clinton's in 2000," *Washington Examiner*, February 5, 2019, http://washingtonexaminer.com/news/trumps -2019-state-of-the-union-address-was-the-longest-since-clintons-in-2000; Ishaan Tharoor, "The Glaring Hole in Trump's State of the Union Address: Climate Change," *Washington Post*, February 6, 2019, http://washingtonpost.com/world/2019/02/06 /glaring-hole-trumps-address-climate-change.

77.  See John Schwartz and Nadja Popovich, "It's Official: 2018 Was the Fourth Warmest

Year on Record," *New York Times*, February 6, 2019, http://nytimes.com/interactive /2019/02/06/climate/fourth-hottest-year.html.

78. Donald J. Trump, "Statement by President Trump on the Paris Climate Accord" (speech, Washington, DC, June 1, 2017), http://whitehouse.gov/briefings-statements/statement -president-trump-paris-climate-accord.

79. See Bob Berwyn, "Can the World Meet Paris Climate Goals Without the United States?," *Pacific Standard*, November 14, 2016, http://psmag.com/news/can-the-world -meet-paris-climate-goals-without-the-united-states; Chris Mooney, "Trump's Exit From Paris Climate Deal Makes an Already Tough Target Harder to Hit," *Washington Post*, June 1, 2017, http://washingtonpost.com/business/economy/us-move-makes -already-tough-target-harder-to-hit/2017/06/01/6bbca3f8-4706-11e7-a196- a1bb629f64cb_story.html; and Brad Plumer and Nadja Popovich, "The World Still Isn't Meeting Its Climate Goals," *New York Times*, December 7, 2018, http://nytimes.com /interactive/2018/12/07/climate/world-emissions-paris-goals-not-on-track.html.

80. "BP Statistical Review of World Energy," June 2018, 2, http://bp.com/content/dam/bp /business-sites/en/global/corporate/pdfs/energy-economics/statistical-review/bp -stats-review-2018-co2-emissions.pdf; Katie Hunt, "In Quitting Climate Pact, Has Donald Trump Given China the World on a Silver Platter?," CNN, June 2, 2017, http:// cnn.com/2017/06/02/politics/china-us-climate/index.html; Nirmal Ghosh, "China, Europe Fill the Gap as U.S. Cedes Global Climate Leadership," *Straits Times*, July 4, 2018, http://straitstimes.com/world/china-europe-fill-the-gap-as-us-cedes-global -climate-leadership; and Edward Wong, "China Is a Climate Leader but Still Isn't Doing Enough on Emissions, Report Says," *New York Times*, July 19, 2018, http://nytimes.com /2018/07/19/world/asia/china-climate-change-report.html.

81. In a *Washington Post*/ABC poll, 55 percent of U.S. respondents believed that exiting the Paris Agreement would "hurt U.S. leadership in the world," while only 18 percent believed it would help. In the same poll, 59 percent of respondents opposed withdrawal. See "Post-ABC Poll: Nearly 6 in 10 Oppose Trump Scrapping Paris Agreement," *Washington Post*, June 5, 2017, http://washingtonpost.com/news/energy-environment /wp/2017/06/05/post-abc-poll-nearly-6-in-10-oppose-trump-scrapping-paris -agreement. The perception that the United States has been withdrawing from the world persists domestically and abroad. See also Dina Smeltz et al., "America Engaged: American Public Opinion and U.S. Foreign Policy," 2018 Chicago Council Survey Report, October 2, 2018, http://thechicagocouncil.org/sites/default/files/report_ccs18 _america-engaged_181002.pdf; Sam Meredith, "The Trump Administration's Withdrawal From World Affairs Is Causing Chaos, Ex-NATO Chief Says," CNBC, October 16, 2018, http://cnbc.com/2018/10/16/trumps-withdrawal-from-world-affairs -is-causing-chaos-ex-nato-chief.html; Kristen Bialik, "How the World Views the U.S. and Its President in 9 Charts," Pew Research Center, October 9, 2018, http://pewresearch .org/fact-tank/2018/10/09/how-the-world-views-the-u-s-and-its-president-in-9-charts; and Robert Kagan, "The Cost of American Retreat," *Wall Street Journal*, September 7, 2018, http://wsj.com/articles/thecost-of-american-retreat-1536330449.

82. Mary Hanbury, "'Industry Must Now Lead': Business Leaders Slam Trump's Decision to Withdraw From Paris Climate Agreement," *Business Insider*, June 1, 2017, http:// businessinsider.com/execs-respond-to-trumps-withdrawal-from-paris-climate -agreement-2017-6.

83. Zack Coleman, "What Has Changed—and What Has Not—Since Paris Withdrawal Announcement," *Scientific American*, June 1, 2018, http://scientificamerican.com /article/what-has-changed-mdash-and-what-has-not-mdash-since-paris-withdrawal -announcement.

84. "Report on Effects of a Changing Climate to the Department of Defense," Department of Defense, January 2019, 4, http://americansecurityproject.org/wp-content/uploads /2019/01/DoD-Effects-of-a-Changing-Climate-to-the-Department-of-Defense.pdf.

85. "Report on Effects of a Changing Climate," 8.

86. Jim Mattis, unpublished written testimony to the Senate Armed Services, quoted in Andrew Revkin, "Trump's Defense Secretary Cites Climate Change as National Security Challenge," ProPublica, March 14, 2017, http://propublica.org/article/trumps -defense-secretary-cites-climate-change-national-security-challenge.

87. Daniel Coats, "Worldwide Threat Assessment of the U.S. Intelligence Community," Office of the Director of National Intelligence, February 13, 2018, 16, http://intelligence .senate.gov/sites/default/files/documents/os-dcoats-021318.PDF.

88. Coats, "Worldwide Threat Assessment."

89. Daniel Coats, "Worldwide Threat Assessment of the U.S. Intelligence Community," Office of the Director of National Intelligence, January 29, 2019, 23, http://dni.gov/files /ODNI/documents/2019-ATA-SFR---SSCI.pdf.

90. Coral Davenport, "White House Panel Will Study Whether Climate Change Is a National Security Threat. It Includes a Climate Denialist," *New York Times*, February 20, 2019, http://nytimes.com/2019/02/20/climate/climate-national-security-threat.html.

91. Michael Brune, "Sierra Club on Paris Agreement Withdrawal: 'A Historic Mistake,'" Sierra Club, May 31, 2017, http://content.sierraclub.org/press-releases/2017/05/sierra -club-paris-agreement-withdrawal-historic-mistake.

92. Ironically, many of his harshest critics are individuals who superintended these failed policies in previous administrations.

93. For an imaginative alternative to the U.S. concentration on the subject of nuclear weapons with Pyongyang, see Philip Zelikow, "How Diplomacy With North Korea Can Work," *Foreign Affairs*, July 9, 2018, http://foreignaffairs.com/articles/north-korea /2018-07-09/how-diplomacy-north-korea-can-work.

94. Kelsey Davenport, "Chronology of U.S.-North Korean Missile Diplomacy," Arms Control Association, January 2019, http://armscontrol.org/factsheets/dprkchron#1993.

95. "Agreed Framework of 21 October 1994 Between the United States of America and the Democratic People's Republic of Korea," held at the International Atomic Energy Agency, http://iaea.org/sites/default/files/publications/documents/infcircs/1994 /infcirc457.pdf.

96. "Chronology of North Korea's Missile Trade and Developments," Middlebury Institute of International Studies at Monterey, http://nonproliferation.org/chronology-of-north -koreas-missile-trade-and-developments-1996-1998; Robert S. Litwak, *Preventing North Korea's Nuclear Breakout* (Washington, DC: Wilson Center, 2017), 12–13.

97. Litwak, *Preventing North Korea's Nuclear Breakout*, 13–15.

98.  Paul Wolfowitz, quoted in "Corrections and Clarifications," *Guardian*, June 5, 2003, http://theguardian.com/theguardian/2003/jun/06/correctionsandclarifications.

99.  George Bush, "State of the Union Address" (speech, Washington, DC, January 29, 2002), http://georgewbush-whitehouse.archives.gov/news/releases/2002/01/20020129-11.html.

100.  Jay Solomon and Neil King, Jr., "How U.S. Used a Bank to Punish North Korea," *Wall Street Journal*, April 12, 2007, http://wsj.com/articles/SB117627790709466173.

101.  Jim Yardley, "North Korea to Close Reactor in Exchange for Aid," *New York Times*, February 13, 2007, http://nytimes.com/2007/02/13/world/asia/13cnd-korea.html; see also Davenport, "Chronology of U.S.-North Korean Missile and Nuclear Diplomacy."

102.  Davenport, "Chronology of U.S.-North Korean Missile and Nuclear Diplomacy."

103.  Davenport, "Chronology of U.S.-North Korean Missile and Nuclear Diplomacy."

104.  Glenn Kessler, "History Lesson: Why Did Bill Clinton's North Korea Deal Fail?," *Washington Post*, August 9, 2017, http://washingtonpost.com/news/fact-checker/wp/2017/08/09/history-lesson-why-did-bill-clintons-north-korea-deal-fail.

105.  Ankit Panda, "A Great Leap to Nowhere: Remembering the U.S.-North Korea 'Leap Day' Deal," *Diplomat*, February 29, 2016, http://thediplomat.com/2016/02/a-great-leap-to-nowhere-remembering-the-us-north-korea-leap-day-deal.

106.  Hyung-jin Kim, "Seoul: North Korea Estimated to Have 20-60 Nuclear Weapons," Bloomberg, October 2, 2018, http://bloomberg.com/news/articles/2018-10-02/seoul-north-korea-estimated-to-have-20-60-nuclear-weapons.

107.  Gerald F. Seib, Jay Solomon, and Carol E. Lee, "Barack Obama Warns Donald Trump on North Korea Threat," *Wall Street Journal*, November 22, 2016, http://wsj.com/articles/trump-faces-north-korean-challenge-1479855286.

108.  Mokoto Rich, "North Korea Launch Could Be Test of New Attack Strategy, Japan Analysts Say," *New York Times*, March 6, 2017, http://nytimes.com/2017/03/06/world/asia/north-korea-missiles-japan.html.

109.  David E. Sanger, Choe Sang-Hun, and William J. Broad, "North Korea Tests a Ballistic Missile That Experts Say Could Hit California," *New York Times*, July 28, 2017, http://nytimes.com/2017/07/28/world/asia/north-korea-ballistic-missile.html.

110.  Rick Gladstone, "UN Security Council Imposes Punishing New Sanctions on North Korea," *New York Times*, August 5, 2017, http://nytimes.com/2017/08/05/world/asia/north-korea-sanctions-united-nations.html.

111.  Michael Edison Hayden, "North Korea Promises 'Thousands-Fold' Revenge Against U.S. Over Sanctions," ABC News, August 7, 2017, http://abcnews.go.com/International/north-korea-promises-thousands-fold-revenge-us-sanctions.

112.  Peter Baker and Choe Sang-Hun, "Trump Threatens 'Fire and Fury' Against North Korea If It Endangers U.S.," *New York Times*, August 8, 2017, http://nytimes.com/2017/08/08/world/asia/north-korea-un-sanctions-nuclear-missile-united-nations.html.

113.  See, for example, "Trump's 'Fire and Fury' Threat Is a Rhetorical Grenade," editorial, *Washington Post*, August 8, 2017, http://washingtonpost.com/opinions/trump-is-playing-a-dangerous-game-with-north-korea/2017/08/08/cafa64a2-7c87-11e7-83c7-5bd5460f0d7e_story.html.

114. "North Korea Fires Second Missile Over Japan in a Month, Sparking U.S. Condemnation," Fox News, September 14, 2017, http://foxnews.com/world/north-korea-fires-2nd-missile-over-japan-in-a-month-sparking-us-condemnation.

115. Brad Lendon and Taehoon Lee, "North Korea Says It Can Make New Bomb in Volume," CNN, September 3, 2017, http://cnn.com/2017/09/02/asia/north-korea-kim-jong-un-nuke-lab-visit/index.html.

116. Donald J. Trump, "Remarks by President Trump to the 72nd Session of the United Nations General Assembly" (speech, New York, September 19, 2017), http://whitehouse.gov/briefings-statements/remarks-president-trump-72nd-session-united-nations-general-assembly.

117. Rick Gladstone and David E. Sanger, "Security Council Tightens Economic Vise on North Korea, Blocking Fuel, Ships and Workers," New York Times, December 22, 2017, http://nytimes.com/2017/12/22/world/asia/north-korea-security-council-nuclear-missile-sanctions.html.

118. "Kim Jong Un's 2018 New Year's Address" (speech, Pyongyang, January 1, 2018), http://ncnk.org/node/1427.

119. Michael R. Gordon, Louise Radnofsky, and Jonathan Cheng, "Trump Agrees to Meet North Korean Leader Kim Jong Un," Wall Street Journal, March 8, 2018, http://wsj.com/articles/kim-jong-un-invites-trump-to-meet-in-north-korea-1520555014.

120. See Choe Sang-Hun, "North Korea, Calling Pence Remarks 'Ignorant and Stupid,' Issues New Warning on Summit," New York Times, May 23, 2018, http://nytimes.com/2018/05/23/world/asia/north-korea-trump-pence-summit.html; and Michael C. Bender, Vivian Salama and Michael R. Gordon, "President Donald Trump Cancels North Korea Summit," Wall Street Journal, May 24, 2018, http://wsj.com/articles/president-donald-trump-cancels-north-korea-summit-1527169994.

121. "Joint Statement of President Donald J. Trump of the United States of America and Chairman Kim Jong Un of the Democratic People's Republic of Korea at the Singapore Summit," June 12, 2018, http://whitehouse.gov/briefings-statements/joint-statement-president-donald-j-trump-united-states-america-chairman-kim-jong-un-democratic-peoples-republic-korea-singapore-summit.

122. Donald J. Trump (@realDonaldTrump), "Just landed - a long trip, but everybody can now feel much safer than the day I took office. There is no longer a Nuclear Threat from North Korea. Meeting with Kim Jong Un was an interesting and very positive experience. North Korea has great potential for the future!," Twitter, June 13, 2018, 2:56 a.m., http://twitter.com/realDonaldTrump/status/1006837823469735936.

123. Helene Cooper, "U.S. and South Korea Suspend Military Drills," New York Times, October 19, 2018, http://nytimes.com/2018/10/19/world/asia/us-south-korea-military-exercise.html.

124. See Choe Sang-Hun, "Trump Says South Korea Is Paying $500 Million More for U.S. Troops. The Deal Says Otherwise.," New York Times, February 13, 2019, http://nytimes.com/2019/02/13/world/asia/trump-south-korea.html.

125. Simon Denyer, "Japan-South Korea Ties 'Worst in Five Decades' as U.S. Leaves Alliance Unattended," Washington Post, February 9, 2019, http://washingtonpost.com/world/asia_pacific/japan-south-korea-ties-worst-in-five-decades-as-us-leaves-alliance-untended/2019/02/08/f17230be-2ad8-11e9-906e-9d55b6451eb4_story.html.

126. Barney Henderson, "Donald Trump Savages Japan, Saying All They Will Do Is 'Watch Sony TVs' If U.S. Is Attacked and Threatening to 'Walk Away' From Treaty," *Telegraph*, August 16, 2016, http://telegraph.co.uk/news/2016/08/05/donald-trump-savages-japan -saying-all-they-will-do-is-watch-sony.

127. Davenport, "Chronology of U.S.-North Korean Missile and Nuclear Diplomacy."

128. See Stephen Biegun, "Remarks on DPRK at Stanford University" (speech, Palo Alto, January 31, 2019), http://state.gov/p/eap/rls/rm/2019/01/288702.htm.

129. Khorri Atkinson, "Russia, China Block U.S. Rebuke Over United Nations North Korea Oil Sanction," Axios, July 20, 2018, http://axios.com/russia-china-us-north-korea-oil -sanction-united-nations-adab18ea-e2ba-456e-83a9-35eb545989d5.html.

130. "Mike Pompeo to Return to North Korea to Set Up Second Trump-Kim Summit," *Straits Times*, September 27, 2018, http://straitstimes.com/world/united-states/mike -pompeo-plans-north-korea-trip-in-october-after-meeting-kim-aide; and Peter Baker, "Trump to Meet With Kim Jong-un in Vietnam," *New York Times*, February 5, 2019, http://nytimes.com/2019/02/05/us/politics/trump-kim-jong-un.html.

131. David E. Sanger and William J. Broad, "In North Korea, Missile Bases Suggest a Great Deception," *New York Times*, November 12, 2018, http://nytimes.com/2018/11/12/us /politics/north-korea-missile-bases.html.

132. Choe Sang-Hun, "North Korea Says It Has Tested 'Ultramodern Tactical Weapon,'" *New York Times*, November 15, 2018, http://nytimes.com/2018/11/15/world/asia/north -korea-tests-tactical-weapon.html.

133. Nick Wadhams, "U.S. Says North Korea Promised to Destroy Enrichment Facilities," Bloomberg, January 31, 2019, http://bloomberg.com/news/articles/2019-01-31/trump -will-announce-north-korea-summit-site-and-date-next-week; see also Biegun, "Remarks on DPRK at Stanford University."

134. See Stephen Collinson, "Trump's Hanoi Hail Mary Failed to Score," CNN, February 28, 2019, http://cnn.com/2019/02/28/politics/donald-trump-hanoi-kim-jong-un -analysis/index.html; David E. Sanger and Edward Wong, "How the Trump-Kim Summit Failed: Big Threats, Big Egos, Bad Bets," *New York Times*, March 2, 2019, http://nytimes.com/2019/03/02/world/asia/trump-kim-jong-un-summit.html; and Jackson Diehl, "You Can't Solve North Korea's Nuclear Challenge If You Ignore Its Torture Chambers," *Washington Post*, March 1, 2019, http://washingtonpost.com /opinions/global-opinions/trumps-flat-out-failure-in-vietnam/2019/03/01/980305f8 -3ab4-11e9-a06c-3ec8ed509d15_story.html.

135. Peter Feaver, "Trump Was Right to Walk Away," *Foreign Policy*, February 28, 2019, http://foreignpolicy.com/2019/02/28/trump-was-right-to-walk-away; Graham Allison, "Misunderstanding Trump's 'Failed' Hanoi Summit," *National Interest*, March 2, 2019, http://nationalinterest.org/feature/misunderstanding-trump's-"failed"-hanoi -summit-45967; Caitlin Oprysko, "Trump Downplays North Korean Denial of Negotiating Terms," *Politico*, March 1, 2019, http://politico.com/story/2019/03/01 /trump-kim-summit-2019-1197242; and Dan Lamothe, "U.S. and South Korea End Military Exercises That Riled North Korea in Favor of Something Smaller," *Washington Post*, March 3, 2019, http://washingtonpost.com/national-security/2019/03/02/us -south-korea-end-military-exercises-that-riled-north-korea-favor-something-smaller.

136. Stratfor, "North Korea, U.S.: Pyongyang Details Its Position on Summit Breakdown," February 28, 2019, http://worldview.stratfor.com/situation-report/north-korea-us -pyongyang-details-its-position-summit-breakdown; David Ignatius, "It Made Sense for Trump to Walk Away in Hanoi," *Washington Post*, February 28, 2019, http:// washingtonpost.com/opinions/2019/02/28/it-made-sense-trump-walk-away-hanoi; Simon Denyer, "After U.S.-North Korea Nuclear Summit Fails, All Sides Scramble to Salvage the Talks Despite Major Differences," *Washington Post*, March 1, 2019, http:// washingtonpost.com/world/asia_pacific/salvage-efforts-begin-for-us-north-korea -nuclear-talks-but-a-chasm-yawns-between-them/2019/03/01/cdd3bbda-3b9c-11e9 -b10b-f05a22e75865_story.html.

137. Denyer, "After U.S.-North Korea Summit."

138. Matthew Choi and Katie Galioto, "Trump Gets Praise From Unlikely Corners for Walking Away From Kim," *Politico*, February 28, 2019, http://politico.com/story /2019/02/28/susan-rice-trump-kim-summit-1195525.

139. Choe Sang-Hun, "North Korea Has Started Rebuilding Key Missile-Test Facilities, Analysts Say," *New York Times*, March 6, 2019, http://nytimes.com/2019/03/05/world /asia/north-korea-missile-site.html.

140. It seems unlikely that Trump has developed policy objectives regarding North Korea beyond meeting Kim, looking good at such summits, reducing tension between the two governments, and seeking by dint of his negotiating skills to persuade North Korea to begin verifiably reducing its nuclear arsenal. If this last policy goal fails, as is likely, the president will have only bad options.

141. The Brookings Institution's Trans-Atlantic Scorecard unsurprisingly gives a grim view of the current state of U.S.-European relations. See Center on the United States and Europe, "Trans-Atlantic Scorecard: January 2019," Brookings Institution, January 18, 2019, http://brookings.edu/research/trans-atlantic-scorecard-january-2019.

142. I am in debt to Henry Kissinger for stressing in private conversations this distressing reality.

143. On the first bet, so far, so good.

144. In this respect, this quote from Charles de Gaulle is especially poignant: "Yes, it is Europe, from the Atlantic to the Urals, it is Europe, it is the whole of Europe, that will decide the fate of the world." See *Oxford Essential Quotations*, s.v. "Charles de Gaulle," accessed March 11, 2019, http://oxfordreference.com/view/10.1093/acref /9780191866692.001.0001/q-oro-ed6-00003521.

145. Cristina Maza, "Donald Trump Threw Starburst Candies at Angela Merkel, Said 'Don't Say I Never Give You Anything,'" *Newsweek*, June 20, 2018, http://newsweek .com/donald-trump-threw-starburst-candies-angela-merkel-dont-say-i-never-give-you -987178; Donald J. Trump (@realDonaldTrump), "The people of Germany are turning against their leadership as migration is rocking the already tenuous Berlin coalition. Crime in Germany is way up. Big mistake made all over Europe in allowing millions of people in who have so strongly and violently changed their culture!," Twitter, June 18, 2018, 6:02 a.m., http://twitter.com/realDonaldTrump/status /1008696508697513985.

146. Donald J. Trump, quoted in Jack Blanchard, "Trump Blows Up Theresa May's Party in

His Honor," *Politico EU*, July 13, 2018, http://politico.eu/article/trump-warns-mays
-brexit-plan-will-kill-trade-deal-with-us.

147.  Donald J. Trump (@realDonaldTrump), "Emmanuel Macron suggests building its
own army to protect Europe against the U.S., China and Russia. But it was Germany
in World Wars One & Two - How did that work out for France? They were starting to
learn German in Paris before the U.S. came along. Pay for NATO or not!," Twitter,
November 13, 2018, 3:50 a.m., http://twitter.com/realDonaldTrump/status
/1062311785787744256.

148.  David M. Herszenhorn, "Trump Threatens to Release ISIS Fighters If EU Doesn't Take
Them," *Politico EU*, February 17, 2019, http://politico.eu/article/donald-trump-syria
-isis-threatens-to-release-isis-fighters-if-eu-doesnt-take-them.

149.  Steven Erlanger and Katrin Bennhold, "Rift Between Trump and Europe Is Now Open
and Angry," *New York Times*, February 17, 2019, http://nytimes.com/2019/02/17
/world/europe/trump-international-relations-munich.html. See also Griff Witte and
Michael Birnbaum, "Trump Foreign Policy Under Attack From All Sides at European
Security Conference," *Washington Post*, February 16, 2019, http://washingtonpost.com
/world/europe/trump-foreign-policy-under-attack-from-all-sides-at-european-security
-conference/2019/02/16/9b1a713a-2fac-11e9-8781-763619f12cb4_story.html.

150.  For a useful reminder of the reasons NATO was formed and why they are relevant
today, see Gregory Mitrovich, "The Mistake NATO Was Formed to Correct—and
How President Trump Is Repeating It," *Washington Post*, February 7, 2019, http://
washingtonpost.com/outlook/2019/02/07/mijstake-nato-was-formed-correct-how
-president-trump-is-repeating-it.

151.  Donald J. Trump, interview with Michael Gove and Kai Diekmann, *Times of London*,
http://thetimes.co.uk/article/full-transcript-of-interview-with-donald-trump
-5d39sr09d.

152.  Donald J. Trump, interview with Tucker Carlson, quoted in Amanda Macias and Tucker
Higgins, "Trump Says Defending Tiny NATO Ally Montenegro Could Result in World
War III," CNBC, July 18, 2018, http://cnbc.com/2018/07/18/trump-defending-nato
-ally-montenegro-could-result-in-world-war-3.html.

153.  Donald J. Trump, "Remarks by President Trump at Press Conference After NATO
Summit" (speech, Brussels, July 12, 2018), http://whitehouse.gov/briefings-statements
/remarks-president-trump-press-conference-nato-summit-brussels-belgium; and Julian
E. Barnes and Helene Cooper, "Trump Discussed Pulling U.S. From NATO, Aides Say
Amid New Concerns Over Russia," *New York Times*, January 14, 2019, http://nytimes
.com/2019/01/14/us/politics/nato-president-trump.html.

154.  Donald J. Trump, ". . . vast sums of money to NATO & the United States must be paid
more for the powerful, and very expensive, defense it provides to Germany!," Twitter,
March 18, 2017, 6:23 a.m., http://twitter.com/realdonaldtrump/status
/843090516283723776; and Edmund Heaphy, "Trump Brands Germany a 'Captive of
Russia,' Days Before He Meets Putin," *Quartz*, July 11, 2018, http://qz.com/1325596
/trump-brands-germany-a-captive-of-russia-days-before-he-meets-putin.

155.  Donald J. Trump, interview with Maggie Haberman and David Sanger, in "Transcript:
Donald Trump on NATO, Turkey's Coup Attempt and the World," *New York Times*, July

21, 2016, http://nytimes.com/2016/07/22/us/politics/donald-trump-foreign-policy
-interview.html.

156. Donald J. Trump, "Remarks at Rally in Great Falls, Montana" (speech, Great Falls, July
5, 2018), transcript from C-SPAN, http://c-span.org/video/?447876-1/president-trump
-delivers-remarks-rally-great-falls-montana.

157. Donald J. Trump, "Remarks by President Trump Before Marine One Departure"
(Washington, July 10, 2018), http://whitehouse.gov/briefings-statements/remarks
-president-trump-marine-one-departure-9.

158. NATO Communique PR/CP(2018)091, "Defence Expenditure of NATO Countries
(2011-2018)," NATO Public Diplomacy Division, July 10, 2018, 7, http://nato.int/nato
_static_fl2014/assets/pdf/pdf_2018_07/20180709_180710-pr2018-91-en.pdf.

159. Jens Stoltenberg, quoted in William Cummings, "'Trump Is Having an Impact: NATO
Head Credits President's Tough Talk for a $100B Boost," *USA Today*, January 27,
2019, http://usatoday.com/story/news/world/2019/01/27/nato-chief-credits-trump
/2695799002.

160. "Brussels Summit Key Decisions, 11–12 July 2018," NATO Fact Sheet, November
2018, http://nato.int/nato_static_fl2014/assets/pdf/pdf_2018_11/20181105_1811
-factsheet-key-decisions-summit-en.pdf.

161. "Brussels Summit Key Decisions."

162. Office of the Undersecretary of Defense (Comptroller), "European Deterrence Initiative:
Department of Defense Budget Fiscal Year (FY) 2019," Department of Defense,
February 6, 2018, http://comptroller.defense.gov/Portals/45/Documents/defbudget
/fy2019/fy2019_EDI_JBook.pdf; and "The European Deterrence Initiative: A
Budgetary Overview," Congressional Research Service, August 8, 2018, http://fas.org
/sgp/crs/natsec/IF10946.pdf.

163. Christopher Woody, "The U.S. Navy's Newest Fleet Is Bulking Up for 'Leaner, Agile'
Operations to Counter Russia in the Atlantic and the Arctic," *Business Insider*, January
18, 2019, http://businessinsider.com/navys-2nd-fleet-to-start-agile-operations-to
-counter-russia-2019-1.

164. Eric Schmitt, "In Eastern Europe, U.S. Military Girds Against Russian Might and
Manipulation," *New York Times*, June 27, 2018, http://nytimes.com/2018/06/27/us
/politics/american-allies-russia-baltics-poland-hybrid-warfare.html.

165. Alan Cowell, "Fort Trump? Poland Makes a Play for a U.S. Military Base," *New York
Times*, September 19, 2018, http://nytimes.com/2018/09/19/world/europe/poland-fort
-trump.html.

166. This outreach comes despite the fact that other EU countries have sought to punish
Hungary, Poland, and others for worryingly anti-liberal practices. See Lili Bayer and
Daniel Lippman, "Mike Pompeo's EU Troublemaker Tour," *Politico EU*, February 11,
2019, http://politico.eu/article/mike-pompeo-eu-troublemaker-tour-hungary-poland
-chinese-influence-rule-of-law.

167. Parts of this chapter are reprinted with permission from Robert D. Blackwill and
Philip H. Gordon, *Containing Russia: How to Respond to Moscow's Intervention in
U.S. Democracy and Growing Geopolitical Challenge* (New York: Council on Foreign

Relations, 2018). However, Gordon does not necessarily subscribe to all the conclusions contained here. See also Daniel Coats, "Worldwide Threat Assessment of the U.S. Intelligence Community," Office of the Director of National Intelligence, January 29, 2019: 36–38.

168. Ivo H. Daalder, "Responding to Russia's Resurgence," *Foreign Affairs*, November/December 2017, 32.

169. Michael Kofman, "The Collapsing Russian Defense Budget and Other Fairy Tales," Russia Matters, May 22, 2018, http://russiamatters.org/analysis/collapsing-russian -defense-budget-and-other-fairy-tales. See also Neil MacFarquhar, "Threatening U.S., Putin Promises Russians Both Missiles and Butter," *New York Times*, February 20, 2019, http://nytimes.com/2019/02/20/world/europe/russia-missile-threat.html.

170. Brian Todd and Steve Almasy, "Russia, Taliban Share Intelligence in Fight Against ISIS," CNN, December 25, 2015, http://edition.cnn.com/2015/12/24/europe/putin -taliban-isis; Thomas Gibbons-Neff, "Russia Is Sending Weapons to Taliban, Top U.S. General Confirms," *Washington Post*, April 24, 2017, http://washingtonpost.com/news /checkpoint/wp/2017/04/24/russia-is-sending-weapons-to-taliban-top-u-s-general -confirms; and Nick Paton Walsh and Masoud Popalzai, "Videos Suggest Russian Government May Be Arming Taliban," CNN, July 26, 2017, http://cnn.com/2017/07 /25/asia/taliban-weapons-afghanistan/index.html.

171. Russia initially claimed, falsely, that the exercise involved only 12,700 troops. Andrew Higgins, "Russia's War Games With Fake Enemies Cause Real Alarm," *New York Times*, September 13, 2017, http://nytimes.com/2017/09/13/world/europe/russia-baltics -belarus.html; and Dave Majumdar, "Novator 9M729: The Russian Missile That Broke INF Treaty's Back?," *National Interest*, December 7, 2017, http://nationalinterest.org /blog/the-buzz/novator-9m729-the-russian-missile-broke-inf-treatys-back-23547.

172. "Putin's Prepared Remarks at 43rd Munich Conference on Security Policy," *Washington Post*, February 12, 2007, http://washingtonpost.com/wp-dyn/content/article/2007/02 /12/AR2007021200555.html.

173. Paraphrasing Churchill, who said, "I cannot forecast to you the action of Russia. It is a riddle, wrapped in a mystery, inside an enigma." (BBC broadcast, October 1, 1939.)

174. Donald J. Trump, speech on March 4, 2016, quoted in "Trump on Russia: In His Own Words," Russia Matters, July 13, 2018, http://russiamatters.org/analysis/trump-russia -his-own-words.

175. "Remarks by President Trump and President Putin of the Russian Federation in Joint Press Conference" (joint conference, Helsinki, July 16, 2018), http://whitehouse.gov /briefings-statements/remarks-president-trump-president-putin-russian-federation -joint-press-conference. Trump later unpersuasively tried to walk this statement back, saying, "The sentence should have been, 'I don't see any reason why it *wouldn't* be Russia.' . . . Sort of a double negative." Matt Flegenheimer, "Would It or Wouldn't It Be Russia: Trump Goes Double Negative," *New York Times*, July 17, 2018, http://nytimes .com/2018/07/17/us/politics/trump-putin-russia.html.

176. Daniel Coats, quoted in Rebecca Ballhaus, "Trump Questions Finding of Russia's 2016 Meddling as He Appears With Putin," *Wall Street Journal*, July 16, 2018, http://wsj.com /articles/trump-blames-u-s-for-poor-relations-with-moscow-1531732220.

177. Nick Burns, quoted in Ballhaus, "Trump Questions Findings."

178. Noland D. McCaskill, "Trump: It's Time 'To Move On' From Claims of Russian Interference in Election," *Politico*, December 29, 2016, http://politico.com/story/2016/12/trump-russian-cyberattacks-intelligence-233045.

179. Donald J. Trump, first presidential debate with Hillary Rodham Clinton, Hofstra University, Hempstead, NY, September 26, 2016.

180. Dan Merica, "The Life and Death of Trump's 'Cyber Security Unit' Plan With Putin," CNN, July 10, 2017, http://cnn.com/2017/07/10/politics/trump-ends-cyber-security-plan-putin/index.html.

181. For more on Trump's refusal to acknowledge the reality of the Russian intervention, see Greg Miller, Greg Jaffe, and Philip Rucker, "Doubting the Intelligence, Trump Pursues Putin and Leaves a Russian Threat Unchecked," *Washington Post*, December 14, 2017, http://washingtonpost.com/graphics/2017/world/national-security/donald-trump-pursues-vladimir-putin-russian-election-hacking.

182. "Trump on Russia."

183. Donald J. Trump (@realDonaldTrump), "When will all the haters and fools out there realize that having a good relationship with Russia is a good thing," Twitter, November 11, 2017, 4:18 p.m., http://twitter.com/realdonaldtrump/status/929503641014112256.

184. "Trump on Russia."

185. Peter Baker, "Why Did Soviets Invade Afghanistan? Documents Offer History Lesson for Trump," *New York Times*, January 29, 2019, http://nytimes.com/2019/01/29/us/politics/afghanistan-trump-soviet-union.html.

186. See also Michael McFaul, "Sorry, But Trump Is Not 'Tough on Russia,'" *Washington Post*, January 16, 2019, http://washingtonpost.com/opinions/2019/01/16/sorry-trump-is-not-tough-russia. McFaul argues that the Trump administration has attempted to pursue a reasonable Russia policy but that Trump himself has mysterious affections for Putin.

187. "Statement by President Donald J. Trump on Signing the 'Countering America's Adversaries Through Sanctions Act,'" August 2, 2017, http://whitehouse.gov/briefings-statements/statement-president-donald-j-trump-signing-countering-americas-adversaries-sanctions-act.

188. Anonymous State Department official, quoted in Aaron Blake, "The Trump Administration's Weird Explanation for Withholding Russia Sanctions," *Washington Post*, January 30, 2018, http://washingtonpost.com/news/the-fix/wp/2018/01/30/the-trump-administrations-weird-explanation-for-withholding-russia-sanctions.

189. U.S. Department of State, "CAATSA Section 231(d) Defense and Intelligence Sectors of the Government of the Russian Federation," http://state.gov/t/isn/caatsa/275116.htm.

190. Alina Polyakova and Filippos Letsas, "On the Record: The U.S. Administration's Actions on Russia," *Order From Chaos* (blog), Brookings Institution, November 26, 2018, http://brookings.edu/blog/order-from-chaos/2018/09/25/on-the-record-the-u-s-administrations-actions-on-russia; and "Treasury Targets Russian Operatives Over Election Interference, World Anti-Doping Agency Hacking, and Other Malign Activities," Office of Foreign Assets Control, December 19, 2018, http://home.treasury.gov/news/press-releases/sm577.

191. Kenneth P. Vogel, "Treasury Dept. Lifts Sanctions on Russian Oligarch's Companies," *New York Times*, January 27, 2019, http://nytimes.com/2019/01/27/us/politics/trump -russia-sanctions-deripaska.html.

192. Kenneth P. Vogel, "Democrats Fall Short in Russia Sanctions Vote," *New York Times*, January 16, 2019, http://nytimes.com/2019/01/16/us/politics/senate-trump-russia -sanctions.html; and Saleha Moshin, "Trump Lifts Rusal, En+ Sanctions as Glencore Shuffles Stake," Bloomberg, January 27, 2019, http://bloomberg.com/news/articles /2019-01-27/u-s-treasury-lifts-sanctions-on-three-deripaska-companies.

193. Jack Stubbs and Ginger Gibson, "Russia's RT America Registers as a Foreign Agent," Reuters, November 13, 2017, http://reuters.com/article/us-russia-usa-media-restrictions -rt/russias-rt-america-registers-as-foreign-agent-in-u-s-idUSKBN1DD25B; Polyakova and Letsas, "On the Record"; and U.S. Department of the Treasury, "United States Sanctions Human Rights Abusers and Corrupt Actors Across the Globe," December 21, 2017, http://home.treasury.gov/news/press-releases/sm0243.

194. Polyakova and Letsas, "On the Record."

195. Gardiner Harris, "U.S. to Issue New Sanctions on Russia Over Skripals' Poisoning," *New York Times*, August 8, 2018, http://nytimes.com/2018/08/08/world/europe /sanctions-russia-poisoning-spy-trump-putin.html; Polyakova and Letsas, "On the Record"; and Philip Rucker, Carol Morello, and John Hudson, "Trump Administration Expels 60 Russian Officers, Shuts Seattle Consulate in Response to Attack on Former Spy in Britain," *Washington Post*, March 26, 2018, http://washingtonpost.com/politics /trump-administration-expels-60-russian-officers-shuts-seattle-consulate-in-response -to-attack-on-former-spy-in-britain/2018/03/26/8ada3d8e-30f0-11e8-8bdd -cdb33a5eef83_story.html.

196. Donald J. Trump, quoted in Kathryn Watson, Emily Tillett, and Camilo Montoya- Galvez, "The State of the Facts on Trump's Foreign Policy," CNBC, February 5, 2019, http://cbsnews.com/news/donald-trump-on-foreign-policy-topics-likely-2019-state-of -the-union-fact-check.

197. Polyakova and Letsas, "On the Record"; RFE/RL, "U.S. Hits Russian Missile Designer With Export Restrictions Over Treaty Dispute," December 19, 2017, http://rferl.org/a /russia-us-sanctions-missile-designer-inf-violations/28927654.html; and Scott Anderson, "What's Happening With the INF Treaty?," *Lawfare*, December 13, 2018, http://lawfareblog.com/whats-happening-inf-treaty.

198. Majumdar, "Novator 9M729."

199. Anton Troianovski, "Following U.S., Putin Suspends Nuclear Pact and Promises New Weapons," *Washington Post*, February 2, 2019, http://washingtonpost.com/world /following-us-putin-suspends-nuclear-pact-and-promises-new-weapons/2019/02/02 /8160c78e-26e3-11e9-ad53-824486280311_story.html.

200. See Kay Bailey Hutchison, "How Russia Undermined Over 30 Years of Nuclear Arms Control," *New York Times*, February 10, 2019, http://nytimes.com/2019/02/10/opinion /russia-inf-treaty.html.

201. It is unclear whether Trump supports his administration's Ukraine policies, about which he rarely speaks. But it appears that, like Obama, he will be unwilling to go far up the escalation ladder with Moscow.

202. Josh Rogin, "Trump Administration Approves Lethal Arms Sales to Ukraine," *Washington Post*, December 20, 2017, http://washingtonpost.com/news/josh-rogin/wp /2017/12/20/trump-administration-approves-lethal-arms-sales-to-ukraine; and Julian Borger, "U.S. Ready to Boost Arms Supplies to Ukraine Naval and Air Forces, Envoy Says," *Guardian*, September 1, 2018, http://theguardian.com/world/2018/aug/31 /ukraine-kurt-volker-us-arms-supplies.

203. John Bowden, "U.S. to Provide Additional $200M in Defensive Aid to Ukraine," *Hill*, July 20, 2018, http://thehill.com/policy/defense/398123-us-to-provide-additional-200 -million-in-defensive-aid-to-ukraine; and Ryan Browne, "U.S. Releases $200 Million in Defensive Aid to Ukraine as Moscow Seeks Better Ties," CNN, July 20, 2018, http://cnn .com/2018/07/20/politics/us-defensive-aid-ukraine/index.html.

204. "State, Foreign Operations, and Related Programs Appropriations Bill, 2018: Omnibus Agreement Summary," Senate Appropriations Committee, http://appropriations.senate .gov/imo/media/doc/FY18-OMNI-SFOPS-SUM.pdf.

205. Ryan Browne, "U.S. Troops Take Part in Ukrainian Military Exercise Before Russian War Game," CNN, September 11, 2017, http://cnn.com/2017/09/11/politics/us-troops -ukraine-nato/index.html; and RFE/RL, "Ukraine Launches Air Exercises With NATO Countries," October 8, 2018, http://rferl.org/a/ukraine-launches-air-exercises-with-nato -countries/29532389.html.

206. Yuliya Talmazan, "Russia's Seizure of Ukrainian Ships, Sailors Brings Muted U.S. Response," NBC, January 10, 2019, http://nbcnews.com/news/world/russia-s-seizure -ukrainian-ships-sailors-brings-muted-u-s-n954581.

207. See Dobbins, Schatz, and Wyne, *Russia Is a Rogue, Not a Peer*. The RAND report observes that "the United States has been slow to erect effective defenses or establish credible deterrence" against Russian interference in Western electoral processes, and that "building a concerted Western response to this threat has been difficult" (9–10).

208. President Obama stated that "it would be irresponsible to walk away from this deal" after negotiations finished and he tried to sell the results to the public. See "Statement by the President on Iran," July 14, 2015, http://obamawhitehouse.archives.gov/the-press-office /2015/07/14/statement-president-iran.

209. "Fixing the Iran Deal: Background and Key Details," http://cotton.senate.gov/files /documents/171013_INARA_Amendment_Fact_Sheet.pdf. See also Tom Cotton, "Cotton Calls for Decertifying the Iran Deal" (speech, Washington, DC, October 3, 2017), transcript at http://cfr.org/event/conversation-iran-nuclear-deal-senator-tom -cotton.

210. Donald J. Trump, "Remarks by President Trump on the Joint Comprehensive Plan of Action" (speech, Washington, DC, May 8, 2018), http://whitehouse.gov/briefings -statements/remarks-president-trump-joint-comprehensive-plan-action.

211. Trump said that "if [my intelligence officials] said in fact that Iran is a wonderful kindergarten, I disagree with them 100 percent. It is a vicious country that kills many people." See Trump, quoted in Watson et al., "The State of the Facts."

212. See Mike Pompeo, "After the Deal: A New Iran Strategy" (speech, Washington, DC, May 21, 2018), http://state.gov/secretary/remarks/2018/05/282301.htm. Among the administration's demands were for Iran to "withdraw all forces under Iranian command

throughout the entirety of Syria" and "end its threatening behavior against its neighbors."

213. David E. Sanger and William J. Broad, "U.S. Revives Secret Program to Sabotage Iranian Missiles and Rockets," *New York Times*, February 13, 2019, http://nytimes.com /2019/02/13/us/politics/iran-missile-launch-failures.html.

214. In February 2019, Vice President Pence asked U.S. allies in Europe to "withdraw from the Iran nuclear deal and join with us as we bring . . . economic and diplomatic pressure" to bear against Iran. None agreed to do so. Quoted in David M. Herzsenhorn, "Pence Demands EU Powers Abandon Iran Nuclear Deal," *Politico EU*, February 14, 2019, http://politico.eu/article/mike-pence-iran-nuclear-deal-demands-eu-powers-abandon.

215. Donald J. Trump (@realDonaldTrump), "After historic victories against ISIS, it's time to bring our great young people home!," Twitter, December 19, 2018, 3:10 p.m., http:// twitter.com/realdonaldtrump/status/1075528854402256896.

216. Donald J. Trump et al., "Remarks by President Trump and Heads of the Baltic States in Joint Press Conference" (joint press conference, Washington, DC, April 3, 2018), http:// whitehouse.gov/briefings-statements/remarks-president-trump-heads-baltic-states-joint -press-conference. It is doubtful that the president's view regarding U.S. troops in Syria (and Afghanistan) is based on a thorough understanding of the complexities and dilemmas of those two situations. Rather, his policy objectives appear driven by the simple proposition that it is better to have American military force at home than abroad, and that U.S. involvement in long wars is by definition wrong.

217. See Aaron Stein, "America's Almost Withdrawal from Syria," *War on the Rocks*, January 29, 2019, http://warontherocks.com/2019/01/americas-almost-withdrawal-from-syria.

218. See Steve Holland, Phil Stewart, and Lesley Wroughton, "How Trump's Surprise Iraq Trip Ended Up Slowing His Surprise Syria Withdrawal," *Task and Purpose*, January 15, 2019, http://taskandpurpose.com/trump-iraq-visit-syria-withdrawal; and Jennifer Jacobs, Justin Sink, and Margaret Talev, "Trump's Reversal on Syria Pullout Meant to Keep European Support," Bloomberg, February 21, 2019, http://bloomberg.com/news /articles/2019-02-22/trump-will-keep-200-u-s-troops-in-syria-white-house-says.

219. A former U.S. ambassador to Syria agrees with the president. See Robert Ford, "Trump's Syria Decision Was Essentially Correct. Here's How He Can Make the Most of It," *Washington Post*, December 27, 2018, http://washingtonpost.com/opinions/even -without-troops-the-us-can-still-have-influence-in-syria/2018/12/27/757582b8-0a08 -11e9-85b6-41c0fe0c5b8f_story.html. See also Aaron David Miller and Richard Sokolsky, "Leaving Syria Is Far Less Risky Than Staying," NPR, January 19, 2019, http:// npr.org/2019/01/19/686489841/opinion-leaving-syria-is-far-less-risky-than-staying.

220. On February 5, Trump said to members of the Global Coalition to Defeat ISIS regarding territory held by ISIS: "It should be announced, probably sometime next week, that we will have 100% of the caliphate." See "Trump Sees Total Rout of Islamic State Group as Imminent," BBC News, February 6, 2019, http://bbc.com/news/world-us-canada -47149088. The Department of Defense estimates that ISIS controls "20 square miles of territory in Syria, down from 34,000 in 2014" (quoted in "State of the Union Fact Check: What Trump Got Right and Wrong," *New York Times*, February 5, 2019, http:// nytimes.com/2019/02/05/us/politics/fact-check-state-of-the-union.html).

221. Eric Schmitt and Alyssa J. Rubin, "Trump Calls for Keeping Troops in Iraq to Watch

Iran, Possibly Upending ISIS Fight," *New York Times*, February 3, 2019, http://nytimes
.com/2019/02/03/us/politics/trump-iraq-troops-syria-iran.html.

222. Roman legions were deployed to Britain for nearly five hundred years. If the president's
critics get their way, the U.S. troop deployment in Syria has only just begun.

223. Eric Schmitt, Ben Hubbard, and Rukmini Callimachi, "ISIS Attack in Syria Kills 4
Americans, Raising New Worries About Troop Withdrawal," *New York Times*,
January 16, 2019, http://nytimes.com/2019/01/16/world/middleeast/isis-attack-syria
-troops.html.

224. Dan De Luce, Josh Lederman, and Courtney Kube, "Trump's Withdrawal From Syria Is
Victory for Iran and Russia, Experts Say," NBC, December 19, 2018, http://nbcnews
.com/storyline/isis-uncovered/trump-s-withdrawal-syria-victory-iran-russia-experts
-say-n950111.

225. David Greenberg, "Syria Will Stain Obama's Legacy Forever," *Foreign Policy*, December
29, 2016, http://foreignpolicy.com/2016/12/29/obama-never-understood-how-history
-works.

226. See Aaron David Miller and Richard Sokolsky, "Trump's Critics Say Leaving Syria
Means We Lose. We Already Did," *Washington Post*, December 21, 2018, http://
washingtonpost.com/outlook/2018/12/21/trumps-critics-say-leaving-syria-means-that
-we-lose-we-already-did.

227. Shane Harris, Greg Miller, and Josh Dawsey, "CIA Concludes Saudi Crown Prince
Ordered Jamal Khashoggi's Assassination," *Washington Post*, November 16, 2018, http://
washingtonpost.com/world/national-security/cia-concludes-saudi-crown-prince
-ordered-jamal-khashoggis-assassination/2018/11/16/98c89fe6-e9b2-11e8-a939
-9469f1166f9d_story.html.

228. "Who Needs Saudi Arabia?," editorial, *Washington Post*, October 15, 2018, http://
washingtonpost.com/opinions/global-opinions/who-needs-saudi-arabia/2018/10
/15/3ebe473c-d0a1-11e8-8c22-fa2ef74bd6d6_story.html.

229. Whether the president's sword dance in Riyadh contributed to his stance toward the
kingdom is irrelevant; what matters is that his policy is strategically sound, no matter
what its origins. See Donald Trump, "Statement From President Donald J. Trump on
Standing with Saudi Arabia" (speech, Washington, DC, November 20, 2018), http://
whitehouse.gov/briefings-statements/statement-president-donald-j-trump-standing
-saudi-arabia.

230. Meghan L. O'Sullivan, "U.S. Is Forced to See It Is Far From 'Energy Independent,'"
Bloomberg, October 19, 2018, http://bloomberg.com/opinion/articles/2018-10-19/u-s
-needs-saudi-oil-despite-talk-of-energy-independence.

231. Kathy Gilsinan, "Why the U.S. Can't Quit Saudi Arabia," *Atlantic*, October 16, 2018,
http://theatlantic.com/international/archive/2018/10/jamal-khashoggi-american-saudi
-counterterrorism-relationship/573148.

232. Ehud Olmert, quoted in Aluf Benn, "PM Willing to Start Dialogue With Saudis, Join
Regional Summit," *Haaretz*, March 30, 2007, http://haaretz.com/1.4813849.

233. See Michael Wilner, "Trump Supports $75M Additional Aid to Israel Beyond Obama-
Era MOU," *Jerusalem Post*, September 11, 2017, http://jpost.com/Israel-News/Trump
-supports-75m-supplemental-aid-to-Israel-beyond-Obama-era-MOU-504800; and

"Senate Passes Bill to Enshrine $38-Billion Military Aid Package to Israel Into Law,"
*Haaretz*, August 3, 2018, http://haaretz.com/us-news/senate-passes-bill-to-enshrine
-military-aid-package-to-israel-into-law-1.6340748.

234. Stuart Winer and Judah Ari Gross, "Defense Minister Welcomes 'Record' $705
Million U.S. Funding for Missile Defense," *Times of Israel*, March 26, 2018, http://
timesofisrael.com/defense-minister-welcomes-record-705-million-us-funding-for
-missile-defense.

235. Phrase from Dexter Filkins, *The Forever War* (New York: Knopf, 2008). For an opposite
view, see James Dobbins, Jason H. Campbell, Sean Mann, and Laurel E. Miller,
*Consequences of a Precipitous U.S. Withdrawal From Afghanistan* (Santa Monica, CA:
RAND, 2019), http://rand.org/pubs/perspectives/PE326.html.

236. Donald J. Trump (@realDonaldTrump), "I inherited a total mess in Syria and
Afghanistan, the 'Endless Wars' of unlimited spending and death. During my campaign
I said, very strongly, that these wars must finally end. We spend $50 Billion a year in
Afghanistan and have hit them so hard that we are now talking peace . . . ," Twitter,
February 1, 2019, 5:23 a.m., http://twitter.com/realdonaldtrump/status
/1091326078323486722. See also Watson et al., "The State of the Facts."

237. See, for example, Dan Lamothe and Josh Dawsey, "Trump Wanted a Big Cut in Troops
in Afghanistan. New U.S. Military Plans Fall Short," *Washington Post*, January 8, 2019,
http://washingtonpost.com/world/national-security/new-plans-for-afghanistan-would
-have-trump-withdrawing-fewer-troops/2019/01/08/ddf2858e-12a0-11e9-a896
-f104373c7ffd_story.html.

238. President Trump stated, "In Afghanistan, my Administration is holding constructive
talks with a number of Afghan groups, including the Taliban. As we make progress in
these negotiations, we will be able to reduce our troop presence and focus on counter-
terrorism. We do not know whether we will achieve an agreement—but we do know
that after two decades of war, the hour has come to at least try for peace." Donald J.
Trump, "State of the Union Address" (speech, Washington, DC, February 5, 2019),
http://cnn.com/2019/02/05/politics/donald-trump-state-of-the-union-2019
-transcript/index.html.

239. See "Casualty Status as of 10 a.m. EST Feb. 4, 2019," U.S. Department of Defense,
http://dod.defense.gov/News/Casualty-Status; and Neta C. Crawford, *United States
Budgetary Costs of the Post-9/11 Wars Through FY2019: $5.9 Trillion Spent and Obligated*,
Brown University Costs of War Project, http://watson.brown.edu/costsofwar/files/cow
/imce/papers/2018/Crawford_Costs%20of%20War%20Estimates%20Through%20
FY2019%20.pdf.

240. Richard Haass, "Agonizing Over Afghanistan," *Project Syndicate*, January 14, 2019,
http://project-syndicate.org/commentary/us-strategy-for-not-losing-war-in-afghanistan
-by-richard-n--haass-2019-01. Nevertheless, Haass opposes total troop withdrawal
from Afghanistan. For less complicated views, see Stanly Johny, "America Has Lost the
Afghan War," *Hindu*, February 5, 2019, http://thehindu.com/opinion/op-ed/america
-has-lost-the-afghan-war/article26176991.ece; Stephen B. Young, "Why America Lost
in Afghanistan," *Foreign Policy*, February 5, 2019, http://foreignpolicy.com/2019/02/05
/why-america-lost-in-afghanistan-counterinsurgency-cords-vietnam; Jason Dempsey,
"Coming to Terms With America's Undeniable Failure in Afghanistan," *War on the*

*Rocks*, February 11, 2019, http://warontherocks.com/2019/02/coming-to-terms-with
-americas-undeniable-failure-in-afghanistan; and David Barno and Nora Bensahel,
"Debunking the Myths of the War in Afghanistan," *War on the Rocks*, February 12, 2019,
http://warontherocks.com/2019/02/debunking-the-myths-of-the-war-in-afghanistan.

241. Originally recorded in Steven Pressfield, *The Warrior Ethos* (New York: Black Irish
Entertainment, 2011).

242. Again, Roman legions were deployed to Britain for nearly five hundred years. If the
president's critics get their way, the U.S. troop deployment in Afghanistan has only
just begun.

243. See, for example, "The Trump Administration's Tentative Deal With the Taliban Could
Return Afghanistan to Chaos," editorial, *Washington Post*, January 28, 2019, http://
washingtonpost.com/opinions/global-opinions/the-trump-administrations-afghanistan
-deal-offers-the-us-a-way-out--on-the-talibans-terms/2019/01/28/b5e45602-231d
-11e9-90cd-dedb0c92dc17_story.html. The *Post* argues that "negotiations with the
Taliban are the only way out of the Afghan war. When Mr. Trump increased U.S. troop
levels to 14,000 in 2017, his purpose was to force the enemy to bargain. Now that
bargaining is underway, the president has seemingly grown eager to pull the plug on the
mission. Last month, he ordered the force reduced by nearly half. That, no doubt, has
curtailed Mr. Khalilzad's leverage. The Taliban may calculate that, rather than insist on
an acceptable political settlement, the White House will settle for the fig leaf of their
assurances about preventing terrorist attacks." However, the *Post*'s policy prescription
seems to be that U.S. troops should remain in Afghanistan until a long-lasting and stable
peace is negotiated with the Taliban.

244. Henry Kissinger, "Eulogy to Nelson Rockefeller" (speech, New York, February 3, 1976),
http://nytimes.com/1979/02/03/archives/excerpts-from-eulogies-at-memorial-for
-rockefeller-an-eternal.html.

245. See, for example, Ryan Crocker, "I Was Ambassador to Afghanistan. This Deal Is a
Surrender," *Washington Post*, January 29, 2019, http://washingtonpost.com/opinions/i
-was-ambassador-to-afghanistan-this-deal-is-a-surrender/2019/01/29/8700ed68-2409
-11e9-ad53-824486280311_story.html.

246. The author defines vital U.S. national interests as "conditions that are strictly necessary
to safeguard and enhance Americans' survival and well-being in a free and secure nation"
and identifies five vital U.S. national interests: "Prevent the use and deter and reduce the
threat of nuclear, biological, and chemical weapons, as well as catastrophic conventional
terrorist or cyber-attacks, against the United States or its military forces abroad; Prevent
the use and slow the global spread of nuclear weapons, secure nuclear weapons and
materials, and reduce further proliferation of intermediate and long-range delivery
systems for nuclear weapons; Maintain a regional and global balance of power that
promotes peace and stability through domestic American robustness, U.S. international
primacy and the strengthening and defending U.S. alliance systems, including with
Israel; Prevent the emergence of hostile major powers or failed states on U.S. borders;
Ensure the viability and stability of major global systems (including trade, financial
markets, supplies of energy, and climate)." See Robert D. Blackwill, "A Conservative's
Prescriptive Policy Checklist: U.S. Foreign Policies in the Next Four Years to Shape
a New World Order," Harvard Kennedy School's Belfer Center for Science and

International Affairs, January 9, 2017, http://belfercenter.org/publication/conservatives-prescriptive-policy-checklist.

247. C. J. Chivers, "War Without End," *New York Times* magazine, August 8, 2018, http://nytimes.com/2018/08/08/magazine/war-afghanistan-iraq-soldiers.html.

248. *Enhancing Security and Stability in Afghanistan*, Report to Congress, June 2018, 26, http://media.defense.gov/2018/Jul/03/2001938620/-1/-1/1/1225-REPORT-JUNE-2018-FINAL-UNCLASS-BASE.PDF. The report argues that "Afghanistan continues to face an externally enabled and resilient insurgency" (22), but this threat comes primarily from the Taliban itself, not from al-Qaeda.

249. Al-Qaeda in the Indian Subcontinent has gained influence in areas in Pakistan as more fighters who had previously been located in Afghanistan have moved to areas in Iraq and Syria. See "Al Qaeda and Islamic State Affiliates in Afghanistan," *In Focus* no. 7-5700, Congressional Research Service, August 23, 2018, http://fas.org/sgp/crs/row/IF10604.pdf.

250. Richard Neustadt and Ernest May, *Thinking in Time: The Uses of History for Decision Makers* (New York: Free Press, 1986).

251. See Rod Nordland and Mushib Mashal, "With U.S. and Taliban in Talks, Afghans Fear They Could End Up Trampled," *New York Times*, January 28, 2019, http://nytimes.com/2019/01/28/world/asia/afghanistan-taliban-talks.html. The above section is drawn from Robert D. Blackwill, "Afghanistan and the Uses of History: Insights from Ernest May; The Second Annual Ernest May Memorial Lecture" (speech, Aspen, CO, August 7, 2010), http://cfr.org/content/thinktank/Blackwill_MayLecture_Aug710.pdf. See also Max Hastings, *Vietnam, an Epic Tragedy, 1945–1975* (New York: Harper, 2018), and Rod Nordland, "Is This the Right Way to End a War?," *New York Times*, February 2, 2019, http://nytimes.com/2019/02/02/sunday-review/war-vietnam-afghanistan-withdrawal.html.

252. Dobbins et al., *Consequences of a Precipitous U.S. Withdrawal From Afghanistan*, 2.

253. "Paper by Secretary of State Rusk" (*Foreign Relations of the United States, 1964–1968,* Vol. III, Vietnam, June–December 1965, Document 39).

254. The draft agreement also stipulates that the Taliban will not allow the export of terrorism from Afghan territory. See Mujib Mashal, "U.S. and Taliban Agree in Principle to Peace Framework, Envoy Says," *New York Times*, January 28, 2019, http://nytimes.com/2019/01/28/world/asia/taliban-peace-deal-afghanistan.html.

255. See Barbara Walter, "Hoping That Peace Comes to Afghanistan? Dream On," *Washington Post*, January 30, 2019, http://washingtonpost.com/news/monkey-cage/wp/2019/01/30/hoping-that-peace-comes-to-afghanistan-dream-on; Lyle Goldstein, "Peace in Afghanistan? Don't Count on It," *National Interest*, January 28, 2019, http://nationalinterest.org/feature/peace-afghanistan-dont-count-it-42732; and Jonathan Schroden, "Getting Ahead of the Implications of a U.S.-Taliban Deal in Afghanistan," *War on the Rocks*, January 31, 2019, http://warontherocks.com/2019/01/getting-ahead-of-the-implications-of-a-u-s-taliban-deal-in-afghanistan.

256. Michael Hirsh, "Will Zalmay Khalilzad Be Known as the Man Who Lost Afghanistan?," *Foreign Policy*, January 29, 2019, http://foreignpolicy.com/2019/01/29/will-zalmay-khalilzad-be-known-as-the-man-who-lost-afghanistan-envoy-taliban.

257. See Mark Landler, Helene Cooper, and Eric Schmidt, "Taliban Talks Raise Question of What U.S. Withdrawal From Afghanistan Could Mean," *New York Times*, January 28, 2019, http://nytimes.com/2019/01/28/us/politics/us-withdrawal-afghanistan-taliban.html.

258. Leon Panetta, interview with Jake Tapper, "This Week," ABC, June 27, 2010, http://abcnews.go.com/ThisWeek/week-transcript-panetta/story?id=11025299.

259. Gordon Lubold and Jessica Donati, "Trump Orders Big Troop Reduction in Afghanistan," *Wall Street Journal*, December 21, 2018, http://wsj.com/articles/trump-administration-is-considering-substantial-afghan-troop-drawdown-11545341452.

260. Missy Ryan, "In His First Trip to Afghanistan, Acting Defense Chief Says No Orders to Withdraw U.S. Troops," *Washington Post*, February 11, 2019, http://washingtonpost.com/world/national-security/in-his-first-trip-to-afghanistan-acting-defense-chief-says-no-orders-to-withdraw-us-troops/2019/02/11/66f913b4-4519-4ec8-9996-c41b9b179c15_story.html.

261. Lorne Cook, "Shanahan: US Will Not Unilaterally Withdraw From Afghanistan," Associated Press, February 14, 2019, http://apnews.com/6a1f4aa311d34e60b7c4962c308d56fb.

262. Ryan, "In His First Trip."

263. Lewis Carroll, *Through the Looking Glass*, chapter 5.

264. Blackwill, "Afghanistan and the Uses of History."

265. Paraphrased from Robert McNamara, quoted in *In Retrospect: The Tragedy and Lessons of Vietnam* (New York: Vintage Books, 1996): 192.

266. This section draws on a forthcoming *Foreign Affairs* article that will appear in the spring 2019 edition (print) by Robert D. Blackwill and Ashley J. Tellis on U.S.-India relations. However, my coauthor does not necessarily subscribe to all the conclusions contained here.

267. Blackwill and Tellis, *Revising U.S. Grand Strategy Toward China*.

268. Conversation with the author.

269. Ankit Panda, "U.S. Approves Sale of Armed Predator-B Drones to India: Report," *Diplomat*, May 2, 2018, http://thediplomat.com/2018/05/us-approves-sale-of-armed-predator-b-drone-to-india-report; and Ankit Panda, "Strategic Trade Authorization: A Fillip for India's 'Major Defense Partner' Status with the U.S.," *Diplomat*, August 1, 2018, http://thediplomat.com/2018/08/strategic-trade-authorization-a-filip-for-indias-major-defense-partner-status-with-the-us.

270. Pallavi Aiyar, "Modi, Abe Back 'Free Indo-Pacific,'" *Hindu*, October 30, 2018, http://thehindu.com/news/national/modi-abe-back-free-indo-pacific/article25364481.ece.

271. Jeff Smith, "COMCASA: Another Step Forward for the United States and India," *Diplomat*, September 11, 2018, http://thediplomat.com/2018/09/comcasa-another-step-forward-for-the-united-states-and-india.

272. See Richard Fontaine, "U.S.-India Relations: The Trump Administration's Foreign Policy Bright Spot," *War on the Rocks*, January 24, 2019, http://warontherocks.com/2019/01/u-s-india-relations-the-trump-administrations-foreign-policy-bright-spot.

273. Niha Masih, "It's Official: India Is Trump's Next Target in the Trade Wars," *Washington Post*, March 5, 2019, http://washingtonpost.com/world/asia_pacific/its-official-india-is-trumps-next-target-in-the-trade-wars/2019/03/05/39000298-3f34-11e9-a44b-42f4df262a4c_story.html; Blackwill and Tellis, forthcoming *Foreign Affairs* article.

274. Kejal Vyas, "Venezuela's Inflation Rate Surges Higher," *Wall Street Journal*, November 7, 2018, http://wsj.com/articles/venezuelas-inflation-rate-surges-higher-1541634089.

275. Daniel Gallas, "Venezuela Crisis: Will the US Target Oil Exports?" BBC News, January 27, 2019, http://bbc.com/news/business-47023002; and Juan Forero, "Hyperinflation Shatters Venezuelan Manufacturing," *Wall Street Journal*, March 5, 2019, http://wsj.com/articles/hyperinflation-shatters-venezuelan-manufacturing-11551798001.

276. Shaylim Valderrama, "Warding Off Hunger, Venezuelans Find Meals in Garbage Bins," Reuters, March 1, 2019, http://reuters.com/article/us-venezuela-politics-trash/warding-off-hunger-venezuelans-find-meals-in-garbage-bins-idUSKCN1QI503; and Peter Wilson, "Venezuela Food Shortages Cause Some to Hunt Dogs, Cats, Pigeons," *USA Today*, May 19, 2016, http://usatoday.com/story/news/world/2016/05/18/venezuela-food-shortages-cause-some-hunt-dogs-cats-pigeons/84547888.

277. Nicholas Casey and Jenny Carolina Gonzalez, "A Staggering Exodus: Millions of Venezuelans Are Leaving the Country, on Foot," *New York Times*, February 20, 2019, http://nytimes.com/2019/02/20/world/americas/venezuela-refugees-colombia.html.

278. Anthony Faiola, "The Crisis Next Door," *Washington Post*, March 2, 2018, http://washingtonpost.com/news/world/wp/2018/03/02/feature/i-cant-go-back-venezuelans-are-fleeing-their-crisis-torn-country-en-masse.

279. Christopher Torchia, "Guaido Returns to Venezuela, Calls for More Street Protests," Associated Press, March 4, 2019, http://apnews.com/f60b33eaf80c462382f2077cafe8827f.

280. *Made by Maduro: The Humanitarian Crisis in Venezuela and U.S. Policy Responses: Hearing Before the H. Comm on Foreign Affairs Subcomm. on the Western Hemisphere, Civilian Security, and Trade*, 116th Cong. 1 (2019) (statement of Marcela Escobari, Senior Fellow for Global Economy and Development, Center for Universal Education, Brookings Institution).

281. Brian Ellsworth, "Trump Says U.S. Military Intervention in Venezuela 'an Option'; Russia Objects," Reuters, February 4, 2019, http://reuters.com/article/us-venezuela-politics/trump-says-u-s-military-intervention-in-venezuela-an-option-russia-objects-idUSKCN1PS0DK.

282. For a powerful critique of Trump trade policy, see Robert Zoellick, "The US Will Be the Loser From Trump's Focus on Trade Deficits," *Financial Times*, May 14, 2018, http://ft.com/content/b6c99a18-5cea-11e8-ab47-8fd33f423c09.

283. Donald J. Trump, "The Inaugural Address" (speech, Washington, DC, January 20, 2017), http://whitehouse.gov/briefings-statements/the-inaugural-address.

284. Max de Haldevang, "Trump Reportedly Called Germany 'Bad, Very Bad' and Threatened to Stop Americans From Buying BMWs," *Quartz*, May 25, 2017, http://qz.com/992271/trump-reportedly-called-germany-bad-very-bad-and-threatened-to-stop-americans-from-buying-bmws.

285. Quoted in Clare Foran, "Trump Criticizes Justin Trudeau, Says US Won't Endorse G7 Statement," *CNN*, June 10, 2018, http://cnn.com/2018/06/09/politics/trump-justin -trudeau-g7-communique/index.html.

286. Quoted in Jeremy Diamond, "Trump: 'We Can't Continue to Allow China to Rape Our Country,'" *CNN*, May 2, 2016, http://cnn.com/2016/05/01/politics/donald-trump -china-rape/index.html.

287. Former Director of the National Economic Council Gary Cohn, for instance, told Trump repeatedly that "if we artificially raise the price of goods because of tariffs we are hurting our service economy." Cohn resigned because of Trump's decisions on metals tariffs in March 2018. See Sarah McGregor, "Former Trump Economic Adviser Gary Cohn Says He's 'Anti-Tariffs,'" *Bloomberg*, May 8, 2018, http://bloomberg.com/news /articles/2018-05-08/trump-s-former-economic-advisers-declares-he-s-anti-tariffs.

288. The moderates have included Gary Cohn, James Mattis, and former Staff Secretary Rob Porter. More protectionist advisors have included Assistant to the President Peter Navarro and, to a lesser extent, Commerce Secretary Wilbur Ross and U.S. Trade Representative Robert Lighthizer.

289. See Philip Bump, "It Remains Unclear If Trump Fully Understands How the Federal Debt Works," *Washington Post*, February 1, 2019, http://washingtonpost.com/politics /2019/02/01/it-remains-unclear-if-trump-fully-understands-how-federal-debt-works.

290. Bob McTeer, "The Role of Foreign Trade on GDP," *Forbes*, May 5, 2013, http://forbes .com/sites/bobmcteer/2013/05/05/the-role-of-foreign-trade-on-gdp/#6f6970b61ae3. See also Navarro's initial assertion in "Why the White House Worries About Trade Deficits," *Wall Street Journal*, March 5, 2017, http://wsj.com/articles/why-the-white -house-worries-about-trade-deficits-1488751930.

291. Gary Clyde Hufbauer and Zhiyao Lu, "Macroeconomic Forces Underlying Trade Deficits," Peterson Institute of International Economics, March 31, 2016, http://piie .com/blogs/trade-investment-policy-watch/macroeconomic-forces-underlying-trade -deficits.

292. Menzie Chinn and Michael Klein, "Is the Trade Deficit a Drag on Growth?," EconoFact, January 20, 2017, http://econofact.org/is-the-trade-deficit-a-drag-on-growth.

293. This paragraph is reprinted with permission from Robert D. Blackwill and Theodore Rappleye, "Unpacking Trump's 'Alternative Facts' on NAFTA," *Foreign Policy*, September 15, 2017, http://foreignpolicy.com/2017/09/15/unpacking-trumps -alternative-facts-on-nafta.

294. The White House, "President Donald J. Trump Is Addressing Unfair Trade Practices That Threaten to Harm Our National Security," March 8, 2018, http://whitehouse.gov /briefings-statements/president-donald-j-trump-addressing-unfair-trade-practices -threaten-harm-national-security.

295. Secretary of Defense Jim Mattis, memorandum for secretary of commerce, "Response to Steel and Aluminum Policy Recommendations," http://web.archive.org/web /20180308153332/http://commerce.gov/sites/commerce.gov/files/department_of _defense_memo_response_to_steel_and_aluminum_policy_recommendations.pdf; David Frum, "Trump Repeats Nixon's Folly," *Atlantic*, March 2, 2018, http://theatlantic .com/politics/archive/2018/03/steel-tariffs-consequences/554690.

296.     Jacob Pramuk, Eamon Javers, and David Reid, "Trump Administration Will Put Steel and Aluminum Tariffs on Canada, Mexico, and the EU," CNBC, May 31, 2018, http://cnbc.com/2018/05/31/trump-administration-will-put-steel-and-aluminum-tariffs-on-canada-mexico-and-the-eu.html.

297.     See Bob Woodward, *Fear: Trump in the White House* (New York: Simon & Schuster, 2018), xiii–xix; and Michael Sykes, "Read the Letter Gary Cohn Allegedly Stole From Trump's Desk," Axios, September 6, 2018, http://axios.com/trump-bob-woodward-south-korea-6239fc9a-e2bf-4fce-b30f-81fd92f0cf9e.html.

298.     "U.S. Exempts South Korea From Steel Tariffs, but Imposes Import Quota," CNBC, March 25, 2018, http://cnbc.com/2018/03/25/us-exempts-south-korea-from-steel-tariffs.html. See Jim Tankersley, "Trump Signs Revised Korean Trade Deal," *New York Times*, September 24, 2018, http://nytimes.com/2018/09/24/us/politics/south-korea-trump-trade-deal.html; and Jeffrey J. Schott and Eujin Jung, "KORUS Amendments: Minor Adjustments Fixed What Trump Called 'Horrible Trade Deal,'" Peterson Institute of International Economics, November 2018, http://piie.com/system/files/documents/pb18-22.pdf.

299.     Donald J. Trump, first presidential debate against Hillary Clinton (Hempstead, NY, September 26, 2016), http://washingtonpost.com/news/the-fix/wp/2016/09/26/the-first-trump-clinton-presidential-debate-transcript-annotated.

300.     Most of what was achieved in USMCA would have been achieved in TPP, with varying degrees of difference (e.g., TPP would have opened up much more of the Canadian dairy sector; USMCA has more comprehensive protections for digital trade).

301.     Ashley Parker, Philip Rucker, Damian Paletta, and Karen DeYoung, "'I Was All Set to Terminate': Inside Trump's Sudden Shift on NAFTA," April 27, 2017, http://washingtonpost.com/politics/i-was-all-set-to-terminate-inside-trumps-sudden-shift-on-nafta/2017/04/27/0452a3fa-2b65-11e7-b605-33413c691853_story.html.

302.     "An Axle to Grind: Cars Block the Road to a Renegotiated NAFTA," *Economist*, February 1, 2018, http://economist.com/finance-and-economics/2018/02/01/cars-block-the-road-to-a-renegotiated-nafta.

303.     Sabrina Rodriguez, "Mexico Imposes Retaliatory Tariffs on Dozens of U.S. Goods," *Politico*, July 5, 2018, http://politico.com/story/2018/07/05/mexico-imposes-retaliatory-tariffs-670424.

304.     Edwin Lopez, "Timeline: How a New North American Trade Deal Happened," *Supply Chain Dive*, October 2, 2018, http://supplychaindive.com/news/NAFTA-timeline-how-USMCA-happened/538663.

305.     Jim Tankersley, "Trump Just Ripped Up Nafta. Here's What's in the New Deal," *New York Times*, October 1, 2018, http://nytimes.com/2018/10/01/business/trump-nafta-usmca-differences.html.

306.     See Jeffrey Schott, "For Mexico, Canada, and the United States, a Step Backwards on Trade and Investment," Peterson Institute for International Economics, October 2, 2018, http://piie.com/blogs/trade-investment-policy-watch/mexico-canada-and-united-states-step-backwards-trade-and.

307.     Donald J. Trump, interview with Jeff Glor, *Face the Nation*, July 15, 2018, http://cbsnews.com/news/full-transcript-face-the-nation-july-15-2018.

308. Gabriela Galindo, "Trump: EU Was 'Set Up to Take Advantage' of US," *Politico EU*, June 28, 2018, http://politico.eu/article/donald-trump-eu-was-set-up-to-take-advantage-of-us -trade-tariffs-protectionism.

309. Donald J. Trump, interview with Leslie Stahl, *60 Minutes*, October 15, 2018, http:// cbsnews.com/news/donald-trump-full-interview-60-minutes-transcript-lesley-stahl -2018-10-14.

310. Donald J. Trump, quoted in Jack Blanchard, "Trump Blows Up Theresa May's Party in His Honor," *Politico EU*, July 13, 2018, http://politico.eu/article/trump-warns-mays -brexit-plan-will-kill-trade-deal-with-us; Kim Willsher, "Quit the EU for Better Trade Deal, Trump Reportedly Told Macron," *Guardian*, June 29, 2018, http://theguardian .com/business/2018/jun/29/quit-eu-bilateral-trade-deal-trump-told-macron-us -france-terms.

311. Dan Balz and Griff White, "Europeans Fear Trump May Threaten Not Just the Transatlantic Bond, but the State of Their Union," *Washington Post*, February 4, 2019, http://washingtonpost.com/politics/europeans-fear-trump-may-threaten-not-just-the -transatlantic-bond-but-the-state-of-their-union/2019/02/04/a874e9f4-25ad-11e9 -81fd-b7b05d5bed90_story.html.

312. See Heather Long, "There Are 'Nuggets of Truth' to What Trump Says About Trade," *Washington Post*, June 8, 2018, http://washingtonpost.com/news/wonk/wp/2018/06/08 /there-are-nuggets-of-truth-to-what-trump-says-about-trade.

313. Bob Bryan, "Trump Threatens Europe With 'Tremendous Retribution' as the Possibility of Massive Auto Tariffs Looms," *Business Insider*, July 18, 2018, http://businessinsider .com/trump-europe-eu-car-tariffs-trade-war-move-2018-7.

314. "Remarks by President Trump and President Juncker of the European Commission in Joint Press Statements" (joint remarks, Washington, DC, July 25, 2018), http:// whitehouse.gov/briefings-statements/remarks-president-trump-president-juncker -european-commission-joint-press-statements.

315. "Trump Administration Announces Intent to Negotiate Trade Agreements with Japan, the European Union and the United Kingdom," Office of the U.S. Trade Representative, October 16, 2018, http://ustr.gov/about-us/policy-offices/press-office/press-releases /2018/october/trump-administration-announces.

316. Jacob M. Schlesinger and Emre Peker, "U.S., EU Set Conflicting Goals for Looming Trade Talks," *Wall Street Journal*, January 14, 2019, http://wsj.com/articles/u-s-eu-set -conflicting-goals-for-looming-trade-talks-11547500468.

317. Jim Zarroli, "China Churns Out Half the World's Steel, and Other Steelmakers Feel Pinched," NPR, March 8, 2018, http://npr.org/2018/03/08/591637097/china-churns -out-half-the-worlds-steel-and-other-steelmakers-feel-pinched.

318. "Factbox—Barrier to Entry: China's Restrictions on U.S. Imports," Reuters, March 14, 2018, http://reuters.com/article/us-usa-trump-china-factbox/factbox-barrier-to-entry -chinas-restrictions-on-u-s-imports-idUSKCN1GQ0PQ.

319. See Lee G. Branstetter, "China's Forced Technology Transfer Problem—And What to Do About It," Peterson Institute of International Economics, June 2018, http://piie.com /system/files/documents/pb18-13.pdf.

320. "CrowdStrike Report Reveals Cyber Intrusion Trends from Elite Team of Threat Hunters," 2018, http://crowdstrike.com/resources/news/crowdstrike-report-reveals -cyber-intrusion-trends-from-elite-team-of-threat-hunters.

321. Nicole Perlroth, "Chinese and Iranian Hackers Renew Their Attacks on U.S. Companies," *New York Times*, February 18, 2019, http://nytimes.com/2019/02/18 /technology/hackers-chinese-iran-usa.html.

322. Damian Paletta and Simon Denyer, "Trump, China Reach Preliminary Trade Agreements on Beef, Poultry," *Washington Post*, May 12, 2017, http://washingtonpost .com/news/wonk/wp/2017/05/11/trump-china-reach-preliminary-trade-agreements -on-beef-poultry. The agreement was implemented in July 2017, but beef tariffs were reinstated after the 2018 trade war began.

323. Keith Bradsher, "U.S.-China Trade Talks End With Strong Demands, but Few Signs of a Deal," *New York Times*, May 4, 2018, http://nytimes.com/2018/05/04/business/china-us -trade-talks.html.

324. Jim Tankersley and Keith Bradsher, "Trump Hits China With Tariffs on $200 Billion in Goods, Escalating Trade War," *New York Times*, September 17, 2018, http://nytimes .com/2018/09/17/us/politics/trump-china-tariffs-trade.html.

325. Ana Swanson and Keith Bradsher, "U.S. and China Near a Trade Deal to Drop Tariffs," *New York Times*, March 4, 2019, http://nytimes.com/2019/03/03/business/us-china -trade-deal-trump.html.

326. Paul Wiseman and Catherine Lucey, "Trump Extends China Tariff Deadline, Cites Progress in Talks," Associated Press, February 25, 2019, http://apnews.com /0104a56ab495461f86cf4883b8d69ee7.

327. Swanson and Bradsher, "U.S. and China Near a Trade Deal to Drop Tariffs"; and Lingling Wei and Bob Davis, "U.S., China Close In on Trade Deal," *Wall Street Journal*, March 3, 2019, http://wsj.com/articles/u-s-china-close-in-on-trade-deal-11551641540.

328. Swanson and Bradsher, "U.S. and China Near a Trade Deal to Drop Tariffs."

329. Wei and Davis, "U.S., China Close In on Trade Deal."

330. Jenny Leonard, Jennifer Jacobs, and Jeff Black, "China and U.S. to Push Back Trump-Xi Meeting to at Least April," Bloomberg, March 14, 2019, http://bloomberg.com/news /articles/2019-03-14/china-u-s-said-to-push-back-trump-xi-meeting-to-at-least-april.

331. See Annie Lowrey, "Does Trump Even Understand How Tariffs Work?," *Atlantic*, December 6, 2018, http://theatlantic.com/ideas/archive/2018/12/the-fog-of-trumps -trade-war/577495.

332. Keith Bradsher, "U.S.-China Trade Talks Face Big Obstacle: Ensuring That Promises Are Kept," *New York Times*, February 12, 2019, http://nytimes.com/2019/02/12/business/us -china-trade-talks.html.

333. As a recent example, President Trump announced the withdrawal of U.S. troops from Syria by tweet (see Mark Landler, Helene Cooper, and Eric Schmidt, "Trump to Withdraw U.S. Forces From Syria, Declaring 'We Have Won Against ISIS,'" *New York Times*, December 19, 2018, http://nytimes.com/2018/12/19/us/politics/trump-syria -turkey-troop-withdrawal.html). He also announced the early ouster of Secretary of Defense Jim Mattis and the firing of Secretary of State Rex Tillerson on Twitter (see

Helene Cooper and Katie Rogers, "Trump, Angry Over Mattis's Rebuke, Removes Him 2 Months Early," *New York Times*, December 23, 2018, http://nytimes.com/2018 /12/23/us/politics/trump-mattis.html; and Dan Mangan, "Rex Tillerson Found Out He Was Fired as Secretary of State From President Donald Trump's Tweet," CNBC, March 13, 2018, http://cnbc.com/2018/03/13/tillerson-learned-he-was-fired-from -trumps-tweet.html).

334. David Sanger and Julian Barnes, "On North Korea and Iran, Intelligence Chiefs Contradict Trump," *New York Times*, January 29, 2019, http://nytimes.com/2019/01 /29/us/politics/kim-jong-trump.html; and Aaron Blake, "Trump's Slow-Building War on Intelligence," *Washington Post*, January 30, 2019, http://washingtonpost.com /politics/2019/01/30/trumps-slow-building-war-intelligence; Donald J. Trump (@realDonaldTrump), ". . . a source of potential danger and conflict. They are testing Rockets (last week) and more, and are coming very close to the edge. There economy is now crashing, which is the only thing holding them back. Be careful of Iran. Perhaps Intelligence should go back to school!," Twitter, January 30, 2019, 5:56 a.m., http:// twitter.com/realdonaldtrump/status/1090609577006112769. See also Caitlin Oprysko, "Trump Tells Intel Chiefs to 'Go Back to School' After They Break With Him," *Politico*, January 30, 2019, http://politico.com/story/2019/01/30/trump -national-security-1136433.

335. Peter Baker, "A Growing Chorus of Republican Critics for Trump's Foreign Policy," *New York Times*, January 29, 2019, http://nytimes.com/2019/01/29/us/politics/trump-foreign -policy.html.

336. President Trump is reported not to regularly read his daily intelligence briefings and to criticize officials who give him information that does not match his preexisting beliefs. See Elyse Perlmutter-Gumbiner, Ken Dilanian, and Courtney Kube, "On Trump's Calendar, Just 17 Intelligence Briefings in 85 Days," NBC News, February 6, 2019, http://nbcnews.com/politics/national-security/trump-s-calendar-just-17-intelligence -briefings-85-days-n967386. See also David A. Graham, "The President Who Doesn't Read," *Atlantic*, January 5, 2018, http://theatlantic.com/politics/archive/2018/01 /americas-first-post-text-president/549794.

337. As Trump put it, "The career diplomats who got us into many foreign policy messes say I have no experience in foreign policy. They think that successful diplomacy requires years of experience and an understanding of all the nuances that have been carefully considered before reaching a conclusion. Only then do these pin-striped bureaucrats CONSIDER taking action." Donald J. Trump, *Crippled America* (New York: Simon and Schuster, 2015): 31–32.

338. This quote is often erroneously attributed to Lincoln himself. See Ingersoll, "Abraham Lincoln," in *Selections From His Oratory and Writings*, 1888, http://bartleby.com/400 /prose/1827.html.

339. Kessler, Rizzo, and Kelly, "In 730 Days."

340. JM Rieger, "'That Was My Idea': How Trump Claims Credit for Nearly Everything," *Washington Post*, February 20, 2019, http://washingtonpost.com/politics/2019/02/20 /that-was-my-idea-how-trump-claims-credit-nearly-everything.

341. See, for example, "Transcript: Donald Trump's Comments About Women," *New York Times*, October 16, 2016, http://nytimes.com/2016/10/08/us/donald-trump-tape

-transcript.html; and David Leonhardt and Ian Prasad Philbrick, "Donald Trump's Racism: The Definitive List," *New York Times*, January 15, 2018, http://nytimes.com /interactive/2018/01/15/opinion/leonhardt-trump-racist.html.

342. Ruth Graham, "The Origin of Trump's Weird Sex Yacht Anecdote in His Boy Scout Speech," *Slate*, July 25, 2017, http://slate.com/news-and-politics/2017/07/what-was -that-sex-yacht-story-trump-told-the-boy-scouts.html.

343. Amber Phillips, "'You're Not Thinking, You Never Do,' Trump Tells a Female Reporter," *Washington Post*, October 2, 2018, http://washingtonpost.com/politics/2018/10/01 /youre-not-thinking-you-never-do-trump-tells-female-reporter.

344. Lance Barron, "'A New Low.' The World Is Furious at Trump for His Remark About 'Shithole Countries,'" *Time*, January 12, 2018, http://time.com/5100328/shithole -countries-trump-reactions.

345. Callum Brochers, "Meryl Streep Was Right. Donald Trump Did Mock a Disabled Reporter," *Washington Post*, January 9, 2017, http://washingtonpost.com/news/the-fix /wp/2017/01/09/meryl-streep-was-right-donald-trump-did-mock-a-disabled-reporter.

346. See, for example, Jenny Anderson, "Trump Reserved Some Particularly Undiplomatic Insults for His Former Top Diplomat," *Quartz*, December 8, 2018, http://qz.com /1489000/trump-lobbed-some-particularly-undiplomatic-insults-at-rex-tillerson; and Donald J. Trump (@realDonaldTrump), "When President Obama ingloriously fired Jim Mattis, I gave him a second chance. Some thought I shouldn't, I thought I should. Interesting relationship-but I also gave all of the resources that he never really had. Allies are very important-but not when they take advantage of U.S.," Twitter, December 22, 2018, 6:20 p.m., http://twitter.com/realdonaldtrump/status/1076663817831153664.

347. Among the most prominent examples of this are his assault on the judiciary, law enforcement, and the FBI; his decision to fire FBI Director James Comey for investigating the Trump campaign regarding Russian interference in the 2016 elections and his attacks on Special Counsel Robert Mueller for continuing that work (Chris Mills Rodrigo, "Trump Ramps Up Attacks on Mueller," *Hill*, November 29, 2018, http:// thehill.com/homenews/administration/418840-trump-ramps-up-attacks-on-mueller); and the fact that members of the Trump family, who serve as unpaid policy advisors, have profited significantly from the Trump brand while the president has been in office (Jessica Kwong, "Trump Family Has Gotten Much Richer Since President Moved Into the White House," *Newsweek*, June 14, 2018, http://newsweek.com/trump-family -members-have-gotten-much-richer-president-moved-white-house-975993). See also Michael D. Shear and Julie Hirschfeld Davis, "As Midterm Vote Nears, Trump Reprises a Favorite Message: Fear Immigrants," *New York Times*, November 1, 2018, http:// nytimes.com/2018/11/01/us/politics/trump-immigration.html; and "Donald Trump Flushes Away America's Reputation," editorial, *New York Times*, January 12, 2018, http://nytimes.com/2018/01/12/opinion/donald-trump-flushes-away-americas -reputation.html. America has seen itself as a "city upon a hill" with a mission to show the world the effectiveness of its model of governance long before the United States became a country (see John Winthrop, "A Model of Christian Charity," 1630, http:// winthropsociety.com/doc_charity.php).

348. Former Secretary of State Rex Tillerson's slash and burn of the Foreign Service personnel system remains as inexplicable as it was devastating. The Department of

Defense is currently led by an acting deputy secretary (Patrick Shanahan); a quarter of Trump's cabinet consists of acting department heads. According to the Partnership for Public Service, 70 of 197 State Department positions requiring Senate confirmation were vacant as of January 2019, as were 14 of 60 Defense Department positions. See Abby Phillip, Manu Raju, and Aaron Kessler, "Trump's Temporary Cabinet and Vacancy-Riddled Government," CNN, January 11, 2019, http://cnn.com/2019/01/11/politics/temps-and-vacancies/index.html.

349. See Steve Weintz, "The Story of How France Built Nuclear Weapons," *National Interest*, July 23, 2018, http://nationalinterest.org/blog/the-buzz/the-story-how-france-built-nuclear-weapons-26381.

350. The headline in a piece by distinguished policy practitioner Tony Blinken asserts that the Trump administration has "No People, No Process, No Policy." The headline is partially right about the first, entirely correct about the second, and wrong about the third. As this report has sought to demonstrate, the Trump administration, for good or bad, has plenty of policies. See Antony Blinken, "No People, No Process, No Policy," *New York Times*, January 29, 2019, http://nytimes.com/2019/01/28/opinion/trump-foreign-policy-crisis.html.

351. See, for example, Gideon Rachman, "Donald Trump Is More Than a Blip in History," *Financial Times*, October 9, 2017, http://ft.com/content/ecfcbf32-acca-11e7-aab9-abaa44b1e130; Eliot Cohen, "How Trump Is Ending the American Era," *Atlantic*, October 2017, http://theatlantic.com/magazine/archive/2017/10/is-trump-ending-the-american-era/537888; and Daniel Drezner, "Will Trump's Damage to Liberal Internationalism Be Permanent?," *Washington Post*, June 11, 2018, http://washingtonpost.com/news/posteverything/wp/2018/06/11/will-trumps-damage-to-liberal-internationalism-be-permanent.

352. The distinguished historian Frank Gavin notes in a private exchange that many administrations get low grades in their first eighteen months in office (Clinton, Reagan, and Kennedy), only to improve in the rest of the term. One thinks of that old Christian hymn, "Oh Lord, for this I pray."

353. Walter Russell Mead, *Special Providence: American Foreign Policy and How It Changed the World* (New York: Routledge, 2002). See also Daniel Feller, "Andrew Jackson: Impact and Legacy," Miller Center, http://millercenter.org/president/jackson/impact-and-legacy.

354. Nick Wadhams and Jennifer Jacobs, "President Trump Reportedly Wants Allies to Pay Full Cost of Hosting U.S. Troops Abroad 'Plus 50%'," *Time*, March 8, 2019, http://time.com/5548013/trump-allies-pay-cost-plus-50-troops.

355. See David McKean and Patrick Granfield, "Trump Is Moving Us Closer to War With Iran," *Washington Post*, February 7, 2019, http://washingtonpost.com/outlook/2019/02/07/trump-is-moving-us-closer-war-with-iran.

356. Alexander Pope, "An Essay on Man: Epistle I" (1733).

# ABOUT THE AUTHOR

**Robert D. Blackwill** is the Henry A. Kissinger senior fellow for U.S. foreign policy at the Council on Foreign Relations. He is also the Diller-von Furstenberg Family Foundation distinguished scholar at the Henry A. Kissinger Center for Global Affairs at Johns Hopkins University's School of Advanced International Studies. He is a former deputy assistant to the president, deputy national security advisor for strategic planning, and presidential envoy to Iraq under President George W. Bush. He was U.S. ambassador to India from 2001 to 2003. From 1989 to 1990, he was special assistant to President George H.W. Bush for European and Soviet affairs. Earlier in his career, he was the U.S. ambassador to conventional arms negotiations with the Warsaw Pact, director for European affairs at the National Security Council, principal deputy assistant secretary of state for political-military affairs, and principal deputy assistant secretary of state for European affairs. Blackwill is the author and editor of many articles and books on transatlantic relations, Russia and the West, the greater Middle East, and Asian security. His latest book, *War by Other Means: Geoeconomics and Statecraft*, coauthored with Jennifer M. Harris, was named a best foreign policy book of 2016 by *Foreign Affairs*.